American Indian Lives

SERIES EDITORS

Kimberly Blaeser
*University of Wisconsin,
Milwaukee*

Brenda J. Child
University of Minnesota

R. David Edmunds
University of Texas at Dallas

Clara Sue Kidwell
University of Oklahoma

Tsianina K. Lomawaima
University of Arizona

THE TURTLE'S BEATING HEART

One Family's Story of Lenape Survival

DENISE LOW

University of Nebraska Press
LINCOLN AND LONDON

Acknowledgments for the use of copyrighted material appear on page xiv, which constitutes an extension of the copyright page.

Frontispiece: Delaware Turtle, a mural at Haskell Indian Nations University, by Eli Jackson. Author's collection.

Publication of this volume was assisted by a grant from the Friends of the University of Nebraska Press.

Library of Congress Cataloging-in-Publication Data
Names: Low, Denise, author.
Title: The turtle's beating heart: one family's story of Lenape survival / Denise Low.
Other titles: One family's story of Lenape survival
Description: Lincoln: University of Nebraska Press, [2017] | Includes bibliographical references.
Identifiers: LCCN 2016012187 (print) LCCN 2016012850 (ebook)
ISBN 9780803294936 (cloth: alk. paper)
ISBN 9780803296534 (epub)
ISBN 9780803296541 (mobi)
ISBN 9780803296558 (pdf)
Subjects: LCSH: Delaware Indians—Kansas—Biography. | Bruner, Frank, 1889–1963. | Delaware Indians—Ethnic identity. | Bruner family. | Low, Denise—Family. | Delaware Indians—Kansas—History. | Indians of North America—Kansas—Ethnic identity. | Indians of North America—Cultural assimilation—Kansas. | Kansas—Social life and customs—20th century—Anecdotes. | Kansas—Biography.
Classification: LCC E99.D2 L68 2017 (print) | LCC E99.D2 (ebook) | DDC 978.1/033—dc23
LC record available at http://lccn.loc.gov/2016012187

Set in Galliard by John Klopping.
Designed by N. Putens.

For Thomas Pecore Weso and our families

Contents

Illustrations

Preface

My family's Delaware tribal history became official in 1626 with the "sale" of Manhattan Island. Many paintings exist of this moment. Tattooed "Indians" wearing deerskin robes, my forebears, meet with Dutch traders, who wear breeches and plumed hats. Peter Minuit presents guilders and trade goods as tribute to the Native leaders. In return the Dutch enjoy a trade alliance. From a European perspective this iconic moment transferred legal title of *Manahatta*, Island of Hills, and the Delawares left. Or did they? Delaware groups persisted through the resettlement of New York City by Dutch traders, the English, and then colonial Americans. Delawares continued to play major roles in the fur trade, the French and Indian Wars, the Revolutionary War, the War of 1812, and the Civil War. When their political power finally diminished, most Delaware people went west along forced migration routes, while some populations stayed in the East. The major remaining clans are Wolf, Turkey, and Turtle. All of them adapt to many different conditions. All are survivors, like my family.

In the 1870s my grandfather's Delaware parents relocated to the Kansas plains, far from Manhattan. Still, Grandfather lived with the consequences of transactions between Europeans and Delawares, as do I. *Historic trauma* is the term that suggests long-lasting effects of grief through generations, and it frames my account. Restoring my family's suppressed ethnic background adds a small part to the marginalized Delaware history.

I am among the uncounted numbers with "Indian heritage" who are doubly marginalized by misunderstandings of mainstream society and by federally enrolled tribal members who denigrate Natives without official recognition. Many United States Indigenous nations are fortunate to have a more continuous tradition, especially those whose members live in remote areas such as North Dakota and New Mexico. Delawares, in contrast, lived in Delaware, New Jersey, New York, and Pennsylvania—centers of early European settlement. After several hundred years of resistance, from the 1500s to the mid-1700s, they were overwhelmed but not finally defeated.

Dozens of Delaware communities continue to exist from the Atlantic Ocean to Idaho and from Canada to the southern plains. Two federally recognized tribes are in Oklahoma and one in Wisconsin. State-recognized Delawares are in Delaware, New Jersey, and Ohio. Others meet regularly, including the Kansas Delaware Tribe of Indians near my home in Lawrence.

Twenty years ago, as an adult, I discovered my grandfather's Delaware origins. Although Frank Bruner appeared to be Native, my parents never talked about this open secret, and his tribe was uncertain. When I was young, he and my grandmother kept apart from our family, even though they lived only a few miles away. As I grew to adulthood, I questioned this distancing. Now I recognize the workings of historic crosscurrents within my own family.

Grandfather's life span, 1889–1963, is an era when lives of ordinary people, including Native individuals, were of less interest to those who recorded history. The nascent civil rights movement had not yet resulted in social and legal equities. Education of Indigenous Americans, overseen by the federal government, focused on assimilation and manual trades. As a workingman, my grandfather left behind no written records and only a few belongings. Among us descendants only brief stories survive. In this account I preserves as much information about my grandfather as possible, from research and family stories. Grandfather Bruner lived a rich, even heroic life, despite prejudice, and I aspire to honor his legacy.

Family members who shared knowledge with me are my grandfather, Frank Lathrop Bruner Junior; mother, Dorothy (Bruner) Dotson; uncle, Robert Lathrop Bruner; father, William Francis Dotson; and sister, Mary (Dotson) Marchetti. Other family members who contribute are my sister, Jane (Dotson) Ciabattari, and brother, William David Dotson. Other sources are family members Theress (McCann) Bruner, Robin Bruner, Becky (Bruner) John, Barbara (Bruner) Johnson, and Gail (Bruner) Murrow. I appreciate the support of my husband, Thomas Pecore Weso, and his family, of the Menominee Indian Tribe of Wisconsin, especially Mary Walker Sanapaw.

Kimberly Blaeser has been a valued guide for this project and also Matthew Bokovoy. The anonymous readers provided invaluable suggestions for revision as well as project editor Joeth Zucco and copyeditor Elizabeth Gratch.

My writing draws on some oral traditions shared by descendants of the Fall Leaf, Journey Cake, and Segundin families. Janet Allen has been especially helpful and generous. Other sources are publicly shared historic Delaware tribal stories and historic sources. Some of the early commentators, such as Reverend Peter Jones, were Algonquin cultural brokers with blood ties—his mother was Mississauga Ojibwa. Reliable Native sources may have Anglicized names or not. I appreciate the inspiration of Clara Sue Kidwell, Ojibwa and Choctaw scholar, who first delineated for me how Native experiences are unique to United States history because of connection to the homeland, orally transmitted literary traditions, nation-to-nation status of tribal governments to the federal government, and identity of tribal communities. These issues are a critical baseline.

My appreciation to those who took time to read and comment on the manuscript, including Alice Azure, Kelly Barth, Mitchell Bush, Robert Day, Joseph Harrington, Susan Harris, DaMaris B. Hill, and Caryn Mirriam-Goldberg. Those who lent further support are Daniel Bentley, Cathryn (Miller) Colton, DeAnn DeRoin, Gretchen Eick, Heid Erdrich, Greg Field, Karen Highfill, Geary Hobson, Jennie James, Donald Knight, Stanley Lombardo, Judith Roitman, Linda Rodriguez, Siobhan Senier, Pamela Dawes Tambornino, and Diane Wille. Stephanie Fitzgerald and her scholarship are a continuing inspiration.

Gratitude to these individuals and many others who help me as I attempt to express personal, family, and tribal experience in the medium of language. All errors and misunderstandings in this account are my own.

Previous versions of some essays in this collection were published in the following:

"Delaware Diaspora Memoir." In *The Fluid Boundaries of Suffrage and Jim Crow,* edited by DaMaris B. Hill. New York: Lexington Press, 2016.

"Silence Is Alive" and "Urban Grandmother." In *Yellow Medicine Review.* Edited by Carter Meland (Spring 2014): 109–12. "Gambling in the Heart of Winter." In *Yellow Medicine Review,* edited by Chip Livingston (Fall 2012): 49–51.

"Winter." In *Imagination & Place Anthology: Weather,* edited by Kelly Barth, 65–68. Lawrence ᴋꜱ: Imagination & Place Press, 2012.

"My Mother Is a Garden." In *Riding Shotgun: Women Write about Their Mothers,* edited by Kathryn Kysar. St. Paul: Minnesota Historical Society Press, 2008.

THE TURTLE'S
BEATING HEART

PART I

A Twentieth-Century Native Man

Frank Bruner (1889–1963)

"Delawares are like clouds," says Brice Obermeyer. "They never get together." He quotes an elder's explanation of the Delaware diaspora, one of the longest of any United States tribal nation. Their first removals were in the 1600s and have never ended.

"Yes," answers one of our group members. This is an annual meeting of the Kansas Delaware Tribe of Indians. She continues, "They may be separate, but they travel the same direction." I laugh. The metaphor works perfectly to describe the stubborn individuality of my family members, especially my maternal grandfather, Frank Bruner. Some years ago I began a search for his Delaware past. I lived near my mother until her death at age eighty-seven, and besides her stories, she left a mound of invaluable documents and photographs.

This early summer morning the Kansas Delawares, related to the Lenape of Bartlesville, Oklahoma, meet at the Wyandotte County Museum, situated among rolling green hills—good farmland on former Delaware holdings. This spacious grasslands region is my lifelong home. Prairies have intense beauties: azure noon skies, fireplace ember sunsets, and an agate band of hazy western horizon where eternity is a real valence. Clouds, as they pass overhead, become personal messengers with information about Rocky Mountain winds one day and Caribbean hurricanes the next. The speaker's cloud metaphor is vivid.

I visited the Wyandotte museum, just west of Kansas City, once before, to research my Delaware grandfather's life. He lived in the area during the early twentieth century, within a block of the original Delaware trading post. After the Ku Klux Klan invaded his hometown in central Kansas, his family moved into this haven. Kansas City's community of mixed tribal descendants had welcomed my grandfather's family a hundred years ago. Today, at this meeting, I want to express gratitude to their grandchildren.

My journey to this meeting began years ago, when a Wyandot student attended my class at Haskell Indian Nations University in Lawrence, Kansas. Like the Delawares, the Wyandots settled in Kansas City during the nineteenth century, before their removal to Oklahoma. My student's family remained in the city. This isolate group knows their Native roots and continues to practice their culture, almost invisible to their neighbors.

In my English composition class the Wyandot student worked hard and often wrote about tribal history. He described how Wyandots purchased land from the Delawares and stood with them throughout the turbulent skirmishes preceding the Civil War. His ancestor William Walker was provisional governor of Nebraska Territory and helped prevent the western spread of slavery in 1853.

This student was among the first people to help me understand my family's connection to larger historic events, including the Delaware migrations through Kansas. He opened my eyes to the cultural persistence of Native peoples into contemporary times. When I was a child, my parents had mentioned the "old country" as an abstract place like heaven, where the past was stored—Irish, English, and German grandparents alongside Native. In their view that history had ended. My Haskell student described a more vibrant history, one linking past to present. From his stories I learned how communities have living souls, as distinct as individuals. When they fracture, losses are real. When nurtured, they grow.

Discrimination against Native people has been so fierce that many people, like my family, suppressed their non-European ancestry as completely as possible. Some black Cherokees chose to identify with African Americans because it was easier. Dwane Lewis of Lawrence told me this and how his Cherokee freedmen family struggled to survive the Civil War and to establish themselves in a farm community that included Charles and Mary Langston, grandparents of Langston Hughes. They also shared Native ancestry.

Traditions do not disappear easily. Today, before the Kansas City meeting, a Kansas Delaware man purified everyone with sage smoke and prayers—in English but with the same intentions as expressed in the original language. After more than four hundred years of contact, smudging with sage smoke, or "smoking off," endures as an aspect of spirituality. The Delaware practice includes smudging the bottoms of people's feet as well as the rest of the body. Another tradition is hospitality. The spiritual leader included me, a stranger with no direct blood ties, without hesitation.

As the meeting begins, another guest, my husband, sits beside me. He is an enrolled member of a federally recognized group, the Menominee Nation of Wisconsin. Menominees, or Wild Rice People, are a related Algonquian-speaking nation. Next to him is the chief of this Kansas City group, Kameran Zeigler, who presides. All Kansas Delawares descend from families who did not make the final move from Kansas to Oklahoma in 1867. Each has solid documentation of ties to the Delaware Indian Tribe of Oklahoma. What they do not have is a million dollars to pay lawyers for a ten-year proceeding for legal recognition. My hosts at this meeting are as disenfranchised as my grandfather.

Now we sip coffee as Obermeyer, the visiting cultural director of the Oklahoma Delawares, continues with the day's program. He researches both written records and spoken stories. As a community anthropologist, he understands how crisp paper with official seals can seem definitive yet create false authorities. Oral tradition can be unreliable factually, especially when the original Delaware displacements occurred centuries ago, or they can support archaeological

1. Great-Grandfather Frank Bruner Senior with fish. Author's collection.

information. History is an imperfect construction, but it is essential to community identity.

First, the lecturer describes how the Algonquian language unites the Delaware bands with other groups such as the Powhatans of Virginia, Crees of Canada, and Ojibwa bands of northern states. Delawares were great traders and traveled on waterways and land trails. Today's highways in their homeland often follow original Indigenous routes.

Obermeyer next presents what historians know about Delawares on the East Coast at the time of the Dutch. He explains how the earliest Delawares never had a central location because they dispersed among waterways in New Jersey, New York, and Pennsylvania. As he speaks, I think of my great-grandparents' small house a few miles east of our meeting. A picture remains of my great-grandfather holding a bass from Jersey Creek. Rivers change names, sometimes only slightly, but always a river is nearby.

Next Obermeyer explains the liabilities of the independent but scattered organization of the Delawares. They never fit into European colonists' patterns of governance. The Walking Purchase, a treaty

2. Delaware migrations. Mid-Atlantic: Precontact to 1737(?); Bowler, Wisconsin: 1822, Mohican Nation, Stockbridge-Munsee Band; Anadarko, Oklahoma: 1859, Delaware Nation; Bartlesville, Oklahoma: 1868, Delaware Tribe of Indians. Map created by the author.

of 1737, excluded dozens of Delaware groups. The Delaware tribe came into existence only in the late eighteenth century in Ohio, under pressure from the United States Department of War. The United States forced creation of a governing body that resembled European models for negotiations. These treaties were primarily real estate transactions enacted by a few people. All the branches of Delawares cannot be reduced to a single group, under one leader, so these treaties disenfranchised Delaware communities.

The speaker's slide changes to a migration map. Arrows flow from New Jersey westward through Ohio, where my grandfather's maternal relatives lived for a century, from the 1780s to the 1870s. Obermeyer says, "Everywhere Delawares lived during their removals, some stayed behind, like in Kansas City." His articulation of this unwieldy history helps me feel more confident about my own research. The arrow continues into Indiana, then splits: one fork goes north, and the other turns south to Missouri, Kansas, and at last Oklahoma.

Obermeyer's final map shows Kansas City watersheds with superimposed Delaware, Shawnee, and Wyandot reservations. "Do not be misled by these distinct boundaries," he says. "These were refugee camps for many remnant groups: Peorias, Miamis, and Christian Chippewas—a band allied with Munsee Delawares. Some Delawares on the rolls were European-descended spouses. African Americans were community members as well." We look around the room and see diversity. Kansas Delawares resemble my family, hues of the human rainbow.

Next he describes religious diversity, from adherents of the Delaware traditional religion to Methodists. On the early 1860s map families cluster in like-minded communities, with some exceptions. I wait, but that is the last map, and the Kansas story seems to have stopped midstream. Obermeyer explains that very little documentation remains for the Kansas Delaware community. "My next project," he says, "is to trace exact locations of Delaware homesteads in this area from removal into the twentieth century and see if religion, history, or other connections exist."

He moves to a discussion of the Civil War era. "Most factions, whether they practiced Indigenous traditions or Christian, united to oppose slavery," says Obermeyer. He explains how Delaware men fought for the Union, as Indian Home Guard troops. The end of the Civil War, however, did not bring rewards. Instead, their neighbors envied their lands and seized them. Obermeyer does not need to detail how the beleaguered Delawares agreed to sell Kansas tracts and move to Oklahoma. This group understands that story all too well.

During the break several people ask about my family's experience in New Jersey and Ohio. When did my family come west? Who are my relatives?

"New Jersey family names include Bruner and Beaver, and Ohio names are Bear, Root, Weaver, Mowrer, and Wolf," I say, "with some Munsee Delaware connections." Several people nod. Wolf is a common Munsee name. Weaver is among the surnames of the Lenape group's official rolls. I continue: "The Bears lived near the Cuyahoga War Trail in Ohio, now Highway 30, and later they changed the spelling to Bair because of German census takers. By then Wayne County was a mix of Chippewa, Mohican, and Delaware groups." I realize, after Obermeyer's talk, how this mingling of tribal communities, refugee camps really, was also common in Ohio. I resume my family history: "A Delaware encampment remained on the Bair land until the Civil War. A family cemetery with fieldstones for markers is still there."

A listener says: "So, your people must have come west just after the Kansas lands were sold. Somehow they found Delawares in Kansas City. They must have stayed in touch."

"Yes, no letters remain, so probably they learned by word of mouth," I answer. "The family first lived in central Kansas, where they homesteaded, with some other Native families, and then Kansas City when that region became dangerous."

We are interrupted as children enter the room. They have learned how to count in the Lenape dialect of Delaware and are ready to recite for us. As they say numbers, I remember we called my grandmother by an Algonquian term but with an English ending, *Kok*-ie. That was the last word that survived in our family, "little grandmother."

Over coffee refills I ask Chief Zeigler, a mother of teenagers, if she knows anything about my Bruner grandparents. "They found refuge in Kansas City," I say.

"Bruner? No," she says slowly. "Bruner is not a name in the tribal archives."

"Probably not," I agree. "They were here after the government made the rolls."

I ask another member who lives in Wichita if his family might remember the Bruners or Bairs but no luck. I am a generation older than most of the people in the room. Their great-grandparents may have known my grandfather as a neighbor, but that was long ago. A new discovery, however, is that Kansas City Delawares are, like me, unraveling history as they live it. Their program includes the capable scholar Obermeyer. I put the date of their next meeting on my calendar.

As a newcomer to this gathering, I hesitate to bring up more personal topics, such as the aftermath of trauma replaying through generations. I mourn the recent loss of a niece to addiction, and I suspect my family is not the only one experiencing tragedies.

As the meeting draws to a close, I appreciate how Kansas Delawares continue tribal organization, even without official recognition. Their history is certain, and absence from a government list does not alter it. Individually and as a group, they value their identity. Each, like separate clouds, floats the same direction, and I travel my own trail among them, on a parallel course. It has taken years for me to understand this destiny, culled from memories of my grandfather's life, my mother's, and those of other relatives. Years ago I began my quest in a Haskell classroom, and I continue to learn more each day.

❖

I knock on the door of a condominium in Laguna Niguel, California, and my oldest sister, Mary, answers. It is 1991. Underfoot are two dogs with furiously wagging tails, not very wolflike at all. They step aside and let me enter.

Mary is in her midfifties and a matriarch with three grown children. I make a fourth—she is my second mother. When I was born, Mary was thirteen and took charge of me. I adored her. Despite our early ties, though, she has become almost a stranger. She left home when I was ten, one of the great tragedies of my early life. We have, nonetheless, a deep attachment. We talk intimately on the telephone almost every week. Now business brings me to Southern California—I will be in residence at Occidental College, guest of

3. Mary Frances (Dotson) Marchetti, granddaughter of Frank Bruner Junior. Family photograph taken in Hawaii, 1970s. Author's collection.

Yuki poet William Oandasan. I have not seen Mary in ten years, so this is a chance to reconnect.

My sister leads me through the living room and straight toward the kitchen. As I follow, I notice her dark hair has only a few streaks of gray. She wears it long and straight, with bangs. She is under five feet tall but large in presence. We do not embrace—that was not in our family repertoire of gestures—but we feel immediate rapport. She seats me at her table, pours two glasses of good red wine, and we talk. For two days straight we leave that table only to sleep.

We converse about parents, divorces (two each), children, siblings, and grandparents. Talk turns to Grandfather Bruner.

"Pop being an Indian made him quite inferior in the pecking

order." Our family name for Grandfather is Pop. Mary is describing our mother's uneasy footing with her wealthy father-in-law, who did not accept his daughter-in-law or her parents. To Mary the reason is obvious.

"He was Indian?" I ask.

"I always assumed he was."

This resonates a long moment, like the stories of the Wyandot student. "No one told me, exactly," I say. I am in my forties, and finally the family origins are clear. To hear her definitive assertion is the first time this comes into focus.

"Our mother tried to advance herself. Indians had trouble getting good jobs and were poor. Marriage into a wealthy family was a way out of poverty."

I remember our mother's obsessive drive to get an education and her pride in her job as a medical stenographer. She insisted that all of us children, especially the girls, train to make a living. Never did she tell me to look for a wealthy husband and learn how to cook. She was a tiger mother before the term was invented.

"What do we know about Pop's Indian family?" I ask. "What tribe?"

"No one knows anything more. He looked Indian; he was Indian." She makes a face. "He was so slow when he talked. I don't think he was very smart."

I am shocked but say nothing. All members of our family have good intelligence, including all my Bruner cousins. I cannot imagine Pop was not a bright man. I played gin rummy with him, and I knew he was a keen strategizer.

"He and Grandmother Cokie were very nice," my sister adds, seeing the look on my face. "Slow. He was slow."

Out of respect I do not challenge my older sister's harsh evaluation.

Now I understand Mary's dismissal of her Indian grandfather in several ways. Some stereotyped thinking was part of the family culture, especially on my father's side. This would not be the first time I heard family members speak negatively about their bloodlines. I also wonder if Mary avoided her own painful past by minimizing her ties. She had felt like a prisoner in our parents' house—indeed, she was household labor and worked endlessly at cleaning, cooking, and child care. The Kansas of her childhood was a place of drudgery. The Southern California of the 1960s, when she arrived with a teaching degree, teemed with glitzy movie stars. She knew some of them. Ozzie and Harriet's grandchildren played with her children on the beach. John Wayne shopped at her grocery store. When I was a teenager, I visited and had seen these figures, and I was impressed. Another reason she considered Grandfather "slow" might be the prairielands dialect. My sister corrected my slow-paced accent, my first awareness of my regional difference as a liability. Also, some Native conversational patterns have a slower speaking pace, with pauses for listeners to create visualizations. When speaking more slowly, storytellers can modulate tones for emphasis. Diné (Navajo) poet Luci Tapahonso describes this in her book *Blue Horses Rush In*. The different rhetorical style can seem tedious to impatient outsiders. Now, years later, as I reflect on Mary's dismissal of our grandfather, these possibilities seem plausible.

During a pause in our conversation, Mary lets the dogs outside to break up the uneasy mood. They clatter to the patio door and lunge through it. When she returns to the table, she shifts to brighter conversation, deftly avoiding conflict. The look on my face is enough to signal disagreement.

"Grandmother Cokie was so much fun. She was full of energy." Mary describes more about this Irish German grandmother who drove a car and made expeditions to see Wichita psychics in the 1930s. Her marriage was, at that time, affectionate. Mary describes Grandfather's joking with Grandmother, something I never guessed. "They laughed together all the time," she says. "He teased her, and she loved it. They were in their fifties then, not old."

"Wasn't he an alcoholic?" I ask. That is the family lore I know, and my second marriage had been rocky because of substance abuse. I have spent some time learning codependency programs for relatives of alcoholics.

"No, his drinking was later in his life," she explains. "He worked for the Santa Fe railroad, in the rail yards. That was dangerous work. He didn't sit around drinking all day." She pauses. "You had the worst of it all. You never knew our parents or grandparents when they had better days. You were the youngest, and all you knew were the hard times." Mary hears scratching at the door and lets the dogs back in. They resettle at her feet.

"I was so spoiled," my sister says. I look at the satisfied dogs there beside my sister. Some traditions continue. "All the grandparents doted on me, the first grandchild on both sides. Mama called her mother each morning to report on my sleep." She goes on to explain how the Bruner grandparents came for early dinner every day, to help feed her. Her face darkens. "Then the other grandparents would arrive in their big car. They insisted on stopping the meal and taking me out for ice cream." She is silent a moment and then laughs. "What child would sit at the table and finish cold peas when she could go to the ice cream store?"

"What a mess," I say. "Divided authority figures."

"Yes, exactly." According to Mary, the wealthy grandfather dictated everyone's schedule. He had already eaten, so it was time for his dessert. No one crossed him. Grandfather Dotson employed our father, so the son had no choice but to obey. In small towns those on top have powers beyond economic clout.

"In those days," Mary continues, "Grandfather Dotson was a successful businessman. The Bruner grandparents stayed in the background. They never joined the expeditions for ice cream. They were not part of holiday meals in the Dotsons' fancy house either." She pauses a moment before saying "I don't think they liked their new in-laws at all."

This conversation gives me insights into my mother's predicaments in her early marriage. She was a strong-willed woman, yet she had to defer to her father-in-law. Her father, a brown-skinned Native person without wealth, had no leverage in the blending of families. "Finally," Mary says, "Cokie and Pop just didn't come by anymore." Grandfather must have understood himself as a liability, as he withdrew from family tensions.

Here is the moment, many years ago, when our family narrative of disruption was set. The alienation of our Native grandparent began early in our parents' marriage and continued to the end. As my sister explains this dynamic to me, the implications begin to unfold. We turn to other topics, to the future. Yet we both understand how we have inherited an inner unsettledness, rooted in this old dynamic.

Finally, after Mary and I have talked about everything, including politics, both of her daughters come to visit. We walk down the street to the beautiful ocean and watch cerise streaks across Catalina Island as the sun sets. The moon rises over coastal ranges to the east. We enjoy moments of enchantment as the day ends. As painful as our conversation has been, it also has started some healing. The natural beauty around us works its magic.

This visit with my sister Mary took place about ten years before her older daughter was killed during a drug-related murder at Lake Elsinore. It was the last time I ever saw my niece. It also was before the devastating trial of the murderer. The judge requested a statement from Mary over one terrible winter holiday. Not long afterward she began drinking excessively to assuage her grief. Mary and I talked regularly on the phone during this tragedy, and I visited twice more before she died. The last time she begged me to leave Kansas (and my family) and move in with her, to be her daughter again. Of course, I could not. Guilt is a useless emotion, but I feel it. Without her mothering I would be a different person, a much less happy person. No one was there for her as family power struggles unfolded.

Mary knew our Delaware grandfather the best and had the least to say about him. Her life pattern, ironically, was not unlike his. Like him, she never found a settled place in the work world. Like him, she lost two of her four children. As a result, she struggled with grief and alcohol abuse. Both died too young of cancer.

Mary understood her Native grandfather's awkward role in a

small Kansas town where his children could find acceptance but he could not. She knew he loved his wife to the end. Mary's stories lead me to believe he loved his grandchildren, even though I saw him so seldom.

❖

After Mary died, I became poet laureate of Kansas, with duties from 2006 to 2009. I began driving extensively throughout the large state, a rectangle of two hundred by four hundred miles. In this grasslands vista the sky can fill a full circle. Two time frames, past and present, comingle. In remote places I explored where my grandfather once lived. After dozens of trips west into the plains, I came to identify Grandfather with the land itself. The sun rises on the rough-etched outline of his form; it sinks into the western horizon with blazes of his fiery breath.

Grandfather is my mythic being, representing all male ancestors. I am not alone in this confabulation. Petroglyphs in the Smoky Hills of Kansas, a region crossed by Interstate 70, often represent outlined Indigenous men—some with buffalo caps, some with feather headdresses, some bareheaded. Most have upraised arms, palms out, as though blessing a congregation or receiving blessings from the stars—or both. The insertion of human measure into the impersonal expanses makes the infinite more companionable. My eyes touch these glyphs through light beams and remember them. The human memory latches onto icons, like a birthing mother, a warrior, or the universal grandfather. The misunderstood "sale" of Manhattan for a few beads represents a conqueror's narrative in shorthand. This is how memory works. Outcroppings of Kansas sandstone archive hundreds of male figures, along with a few women, many animals, stars, and water glyphs.

During one excursion to Hill City in 2008, to celebrate the poet William Stafford, I travel to an anthropomorphic outline of stones in far western Kansas known as Penokee Man. This archetypal man suggests all grandfathers. To my children and grandchildren our Grandfather Bruner is no more real than this roughly delineated

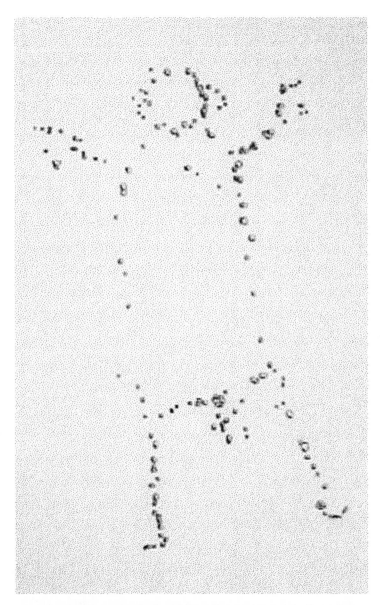

4. Penokee Man drawing in Graham County Historical Society, by Donna Roper, after a map by Tom Witty in the Kansas State Historical Society collection, 1978. Used with permission of Graham County Historical Society of Hill City, Kansas. The author appreciates the cooperation of Jan Beecher.

image, which diminishes each year as it weathers. Grandfather's memory fades, but he is, nonetheless, a powerful if unconscious presence in our flesh and bones.

The hundreds-year-old giant Penokee Man stretches sixty feet across a hillside. He has broad shoulders, barrel chest, and large penis. He raises his arms in the same open gesture of petroglyph men found in the Smoky Hills. His feet straddle the evening sun, and at the summer solstice the sun's orb fits exactly between his legs. Individual pieces barely suggest the whole image, yet from the air he is complete. The large outline is an apt creation for this place of unedged sky. His scale challenges people to reach for a larger view.

Penokee Man is also a sundial. Passersby experience his calibration of time as an ongoing, organic process. Yearly deteriorations of the stones extend the past into the present. Each follows a specific, long-range clock, marking a sequence unique to Ogallala sediments. A nearby outcropping of Ogallala sandstone is the source for the outlined man. The seam runs underground into a deep reservoir of Ice Age groundwater. Exposed to the elements, the broken fragments of stone turn to gravel and then clay. I observe discrete segments of this process in my pane of time.

Anthropologists connect Penokee Man to Blackfeet Indians' Old Man, the world's cocreator with Old Woman. Blackfeet people are the most far-flung branch of Algonquian-speaking people, settled on slopes of the northern Rocky Mountains. According to Blackfeet accounts, Penokee Man is a cosmic grandfather with many children, from the southern plains northward to Montana:

> Old Man came from the south, making the mountains, the prairies, and the forests as he passed along, making the birds and the animals also. He traveled northward making things as he went, putting red paint in the ground here and there—arranging the world as we see it today. He made the Milk River and crossed it; being tired, he went up on a little hill and lay down to rest. As he lay on his back, stretched out on the grass with his arms

extended, he marked his figure with stones. You can see those rocks today, they show the shape of his body, legs, arms and hair. (Chewing Black Bones)

These distant relatives of my grandfather left Penokee Man, a figure complete with "body, legs, arms and hair."

The connection to Grandfather deepens as I remember how he once lived in Norton County, a few miles from Penokee Man, and most likely he visited the site. Perhaps our footsteps crisscross, separated only by years.

As I drive away from Penokee Man, toward home, I learn another landscape—breaks country. Entire communities fit into breaks, which are steep drop-offs into canyons. From a distance the land looks like even rolling hills, but suddenly the earth cracks open and drops to a small stream. This high plains region is an unfolding atlas, where creases can conceal hundreds of miles.

The highway parallels a valley as it wends among giant swells. In Norton County the road eases its way through the long-term erosion site of Prairie Dog Creek. This is also a former stagecoach trail. Remnants of livery stables remain in some of the small towns. No doubt the passage was a way for Blackfeet and other Native peoples to travel the region. The Blackfeet elder Darrell Kipp once told me about the long-range raids the warriors made, south as far as Mexico and back.

Anything can happen in such distant places, where time and space converge. When a child, I watched the film *Lost Horizons*, and the term stays with me. Shangri-La can become real at any turn on the road.

After I arrive home, I still feel enlarged by the larger scale of experience, an immersion in a rock fissure where history stands still. As I continue these statewide drives during poet laureate days, Grandfather is more and more real to me. I plan side trips to places where he once lived—the oil fields of Butler County, Santa Fe railroad towns, and endless pastures. In his small hometowns brick streets map exact dimensions of his former life. The Methodist church, the railroad depot, an old office building, a Carnegie library—they all take on an added magnetism as I drive past them or stop for longer investigation.

Through these years my writing style picks up a more exploratory, rambling quality. All writing is a form of travel memoir anyway, as we traverse our own memories and add new observations. Exceptional writers can make quotidian, rote moments into heroic epics. My journal entries about road trips turn into imaginative journeys, and some moments solidify into published pages.

To be accurate about these trips, I have to describe what I observe, not what I wish to see. Kansas, like my family, with its inconsistencies, is not a perfect place. Seedy motel rooms overlook fields of gorgeous wildflowers. Rusted cars litter some Edenic hillsides. Metal utility buildings hunch wherever they wish, as picturesque red barns collapse into rubble. The eternal skies, however, make everything human-made seem as temporary as dried cottonwood leaves. The stunning beauty of land never fails to transcend scars, human and natural. Natural theology becomes my personal creed, observation of the invariable laws of gravity, light, electricity, and velocity. Penokee Man works on my imagination and expands it as well as the mysterious optics of the breaks country.

Traveling, an elder once told me, is a Delaware tradition. Delawares traversed the Atlantic Seaboard, the Great Lakes, and the West as traders and guides. The remarkable Delaware man Fall Leaf led Zebulon Pike to the tallest peak in the Rockies. The landmark should be named Fall Leaf's Peak, not Pike's Peak. Pike only followed the Delaware man's lead.

Grandfather also traveled widely. As a boy, he visited New Mexico cousins to hunt and fish in mountain streams. These cousins returned with him to Kansas, to renew ties with their Delaware grandparents. Grandfather's sojourns in New Mexico and Norton County are part of a larger whole, still existing in a fourth dimension where the past is a complete single cloth.

Grandfather's blood lineage flows back to many great-grandparents before us who survived with great courage. We descendants continue their ongoing creation, just as the sun illumines, each sunrise, the image of Penokee Man. On the plains distances expand and contract, so at times even the stars seem within an arm's reach of the earth.

❖

Not long after my sister Mary informs me about our Grandfather's Native identity, I drive to his hometown of Burns, northeast of Wichita. A cousin has given me the name of an old woman who knew my grandfather's relatives. The land is diverse, with oil fields, upland pastures, and farming along river bottoms.

Just after the cemetery, the turnoff to Burns leads beyond the edge of the Cottonwood River. A gas station is 1960s throwback architecture, then brick streets converge on nineteenth-century downtown buildings. Some are quite ornate, suggesting a former age of glory. Prosperity once blew through the town like a spring storm and left some embellished rooflines. In the aftermath utility buildings and wood-frame storefronts fill in the remaining spaces. The town is a jumble of eras.

I find the address of a white Victorian house with petunia-filled flower boxes on the front steps. An old woman answers the door promptly. She is a fit octogenarian with tea ready. After pouring and offering store-bought cookies, with apologies, she settles into her overstuffed chair and says, "So, you are Charley Bruner's great-niece." I nod, and she continues, "He was a banker in town all those years." Grandfather's brother married an energetic woman, a schoolteacher, and in the small town they became prominent. "He kept the Boy Scouts going for years," she says. "Your Aunt Hazel was a poet with the Kansas Author's Club." I have heard of this literary relative by marriage, one of my mother's favorites. She loved the outdoors and would disappear all day into the hills and "commune with nature," my mother said. This woman corroborates my mother's stories.

5. Frank Bruner Junior, age fifteen or sixteen, at railroad crossing in Burns, Kansas. Author's collection.

My hostess sips her tea and says: "I don't know much about your grandfather. He wandered so much, from Kansas City to California and back."

"I thought he just lived in Newton," I say.

"He ended up in Newton after the war." "The war" is always World War II for people of her age. She takes up her teacup again, looks at me, and then confides, "I worked in the Bruner dulcimer factory awhile."

Small isolated towns look for any possible way to develop business. My mother had mentioned her cousin and this unusual enterprise, but I did not realize he employed anybody. "I heard about the Walnut Creek Dulcimer Factory," I say.

"Yup. It went out of business. Your cousin moved to Oklahoma a year ago." I had not heard this coda to the tale.

"Oh, no," I say.

"Your cousin, he was a real character."

I understand her colloquial shorthand for very eccentric and intelligent and interesting and, again, very eccentric, all at once. Most differences are forgiven with this endearment. Many "real characters" inhabit small Kansas towns. With luck I might become a real character myself.

She spends the afternoon sharing her uncensored opinions. She describes former triumphs of the town, including the first consolidated school district in the state. "There were fun times," the elder tells me. She describes how teenagers played sports and celebrated picnic holidays with cakewalks and tug-of-war. Youngsters gathered at the railroad crossings, my grandfather among them, and shot targets.

She knows the exact house where my great-uncle lived, the bank where he worked, and the drugstore where he ate lunch. She tells me about Grandmother Charlotte, my grandfather's mother, who was a widow when this woman was young: "She might have been Indian. She looked it. But no one talked about those things." Grandmother Charlotte, she intimates, also was a real character who lived with her son and daughter-in-law until she died in 1954.

"You can see for yourself what's left at the town museum," she says to me. "Just go a few streets over to the old high school building. I called for someone to unlock it."

I thank her for tea and take my leave.

The large, square brick high school building is not difficult to find in a town six blocks wide. I climb steep concrete stairs to the entrance. Upon entering, I see this is a doubly abandoned building—no longer a high school and no longer the town museum. Dust and cobwebs are thick. In the entrance hall locked glass cases display rows of trophies, with each former victory neatly labeled. The young athletes are long absent, as are the teachers, parents, janitors, and classmates. The transience of glory is an explicit lesson as photographs fade to gray outlines.

Classrooms are display areas for town antiques. One room is filled with Victorian dresses, another with china plates and glassware. Photographs create a jumbled mound on one table. I look for anything about my family as quickly as possible, so I can finish

6. Two brothers: Charles Bruner and Frank Junior in bow ties, 1895–1900, Burns, Kansas, area. Author's collection. Gift of Gail Bruner Murrow.

7. Burns State Bank, ca. 1900–1909. Samuel E. Cobb (*right*), Charles Bruner (*back*), and Theo Cobb, daughter of Samuel Cobb, who became wife of Alf Landon. Landon was twenty-sixth governor of Kansas and opponent of Franklin D. Roosevelt in 1936. Author's collection.

and leave this spooky place. Among the photos I see several my mother already has. Finally, I discover one new photograph of Grandfather's older brothers, dressed like dandies. They look a bit ridiculous now, especially in puffy necktie bows, but no doubt they were fashion plates.

Another photograph shows the older brother, Charles, as a young clerk with a prominent banker, Samuel E. Cobb, grandfather of former senator Nancy Landon Kassebaum. Nancy's mother, Theo (Landon) Cobb, is a small girl in the photo. Among the paper rubble I also find a town history that quotes Cobb, founder of the bank: "My mother died when I was about three years old. . . . I made my first fifty cents hoeing hedges." Cobb became the first mayor of Burns, despite his humble origins. Another large photograph of Cobb is a formal portrait. He has a broad, handsome face. His dark complexion partly merges with shadows. He appears to be American Indian. The history article explains that Cobb left Burns in 1909 for Topeka to become a prominent citizen. Uncle Charles bought the bank and stayed in Burns until his death in 1971. His wealth, like Cobb's, came from hard work, not family fortune.

On a side table I find some regional books for sale. One volume is a compilation of centennial memories, and the other is reprinted newspaper clippings. I tuck bills in the on-your-honor collection jar. The local histories will prove my family did exist in this dip in the horizon, a place that prospered as citizens waited futilely for the train company to establish a major route to Kansas City. This community still waits in its wrinkle of the grasslands.

I trudge back down the steep high school building steps to my car. On the way out of town, I make one last stop, the Burns Café and Bakery, for a sacramental meal of rhubarb pie and coffee. The lingering tartness of the fruit transforms the drive home through the Flint Hills into a religious experience. Shadows of misty ridgelines blend into the horizon, and the past swirls into present time as I contemplate the childhood days of Grandfather in this landscape of constant change.

❖

I open pages of the Burns centennial history and discover how my grandfather's life began. The *Burns Monitor* reports his birth in 1889: "Mrs. F. L. Bruner presented her husband with a 10-lb. boy as a Christmas present." Frank Bruner Junior was the third and last child. The town was at its height, as prospering ranchers and farmers accrued solid accounts in the local bank. The new baby's father was a postmaster and a clerk. At first the Bruner family flourished in the hometown setting, with grandparents, uncles, aunts, and cousins nearby. They all were among the founding families, if not exactly prominent citizens.

The Burns history book lists the Bruner family as arriving in 1878, the same year as Grandfather's mother's family, the Roots and Bairs. All had Delaware ties, not recorded in the public documents.

Grandfather's father, Frank Bruner Senior, had origins in New Jersey. He was born in 1859 and arrived in Burns with his parents,

8. Frank Bruner Senior as a young man. Author's collection. Gift of Gail Bruner Murrow.

Jake and Mary. His romance with Charlotte Root, newly arrived from Ohio, is easy to imagine. No story remains, but Charlotte lived within a few blocks of the small business district where he worked. They met and married. They had a child by 1885, another one in 1887, and my grandfather in 1889.

When Grandfather was born, his cowboy grandfather Jake, legally Charles Jacob Bruner, lived ten miles outside of town. He had remarried after his children's mother died in 1884, and some family estrangement is apparent. At Jake's death in 1912, the second wife's name appears on the ranch plat maps, so Jake's children were disinherited, or the land may have been hers before marriage. In historic records only one mention occurs: "Among those who developed the livestock industry during the early days were . . . C. F. [*sic*] Bruner." He did not participate in town activities, so probably he spent most of his days in the country.

A photograph remains of Jake Bruner with his son, Frank Senior, and another man, possibly a son-in-law. Jake is dressed in worn boots and holds his cowboy hat in his hand, a contrast to Frank's city garb—a three-piece suit. Frank, according to my mother, was sickly and not able to work on the ranch. He had "rose fever," the term for allergies. In this family photograph he has delicate features. In contrast, the father, Jake, has a ragged beard and a hard look in his eye. Jake emigrated from mountain country adjacent to the present-day Ramapough Lenape Indian Reservation in New Jersey. The 1860 census records indicate he owned nothing in New Jersey, he was a day laborer, and he was illiterate. No record of service during the Civil War remains, and his whereabouts then are unknown. Family stories suggest several of his children died in New Jersey. The missing stories nag at me. Why would Jake and his wife, Mary, leave their homes in middle age and chance the hard country of the Great Plains? Within a few years Mary died. Perhaps she had tuberculosis and went west for the low humidity. Perhaps she grieved dead children.

By the time of the 1900 census in Kansas, Jake farmed and ranched on mortgaged land. Hard rural work is the same, no matter what the geography.

Closer to the new Bruner baby's family, a few blocks away, were the maternal grandparents, Samuel Root and Mary Ann Bair—her maiden name is spelled *Bear* in the Ohio records, *Bare*, and finally *Bair*. Some censuses show her as "Indian," and Samuel's mother also is indicated as Indian in Ohio census records. This family lived on the edge of Burns and had farmland farther south where they raised seven children. By the time Grandfather was born, they had many grandchildren. Later a neighbor would write about Sam Root's nearby cherry and apple orchard in the town history book, how "children chose it as a favorite place for climbing." Some of the apples went into rural staples of vinegar and cider, including hard cider. Apple growing was part of the family's Ohio experience. Near their land was a Delaware settlement called "Chauquecake," which means "Apple Orchard." They continued orchard cultivation in Burns.

The Root family homestead is still desirable—uplands for pasturing cattle and fertile lowlands for raising forage and wheat. Variety offsets variable weather conditions. The Root family did well enough. A picture survives of the Root brothers as young men, smiling and confident. They wear rough wool trousers, vests, overcoats, and hats—newsboy flat caps and Homburgs. They are informal, and no fake Greek columns are in the photograph. They pose together in a close clump. A few years later most of the Root siblings, Great-Grandmother Charlotte among them, pose together again. The Root family members were close.

So, for his early years Grandfather lived within the shelter of his mother's extended family. He had the freedom to visit the nearby orchard and his grandparents' farmhouse. The region is still a child's paradise. Deer, raccoon, black squirrels, rabbits, and garter snakes live in yards as well as fields. This is the center of the North American flyway, where huge flocks flow north and south with the seasons. Wild turkey gather along roadsides, feeding on seeds, worms, insects, and rodents. Coyotes fill the ecological niche of wolves, and their evening conversations echo the valleys. Ornate box turtles slog deliberately through tall grass, carrying their yellow-striped shells and peering at the world through red eyes (male) or brown (female).

At that moment perhaps Burns was an idyllic place. It is on a branch of the Chisholm Trail, now Route 77. Homesteaders included a mix of eastern immigrant tribal people like Delawares. Families of Southeast tribes, especially Cherokee and Choctaw, also moved into the plains as well as Exodusters and immigrants from the British

Isles, Czechoslovakia, Germany, and Russia. Perhaps everyone got along. Several Kansan residents have told me this was a part of the country and a time when people considered "colored" or "mulatto" or "Indian" could blend in, especially in the rural areas. In Lawrence, a hundred miles east, the writer Langston Hughes's multiracial grandparents appear in the 1870 census as white. They owned property, they were educated, and they were industrious—the cultural definition of "white" at the time.

A shift occurred by the end of the nineteenth century, as census takers specified "race" more strictly. The Langstons are identified as "mulatto" in 1880, and then in the next decade they are "colored." Relatives tell me that this process occurred in the Burns area as well, with less and less tolerance for ethnicities other than Protestant and northern European. My relatives gradually disappear from the town histories, except for Great Uncle Charles, whose bank and prominent wife secured his position.

In 1889, when Grandfather was born, the small Kansas town was a safe and rich environment. He received a good education, and he learned ranching skills from his grandparents and uncles. The land itself is another, more exacting teacher, with inviolable laws of gravity, heat, and velocity. When Grandfather was a teenager, 489 people lived in Burns. Today about 200 people remain. Some nearby town sites are complete ghost towns, with all the population in cemeteries. They travel silently into the next layer of sod as barns disassemble and frost heaves the last paving stones. Time is the most precise law of all.

❖

With a giant map of Kansas, I travel one hot, windy afternoon on back highways of the Flint Hills. I seek graves of my grandfather's paternal grandparents, Jake and Mary E. Bruner. I hope to learn something of this couple, who were raised near the Ramapough band of Delawares. My grandfather knew his grandfather Jake Bruner while growing up, but his grandmother Mary E. Bruner was in the grave by the time he was born. No one spoke to me about these

9. Jacob and Mary Bruner's tombstone in rural northern Butler County, Kansas. Photograph taken 2013. Author's collection.

relatives from a mixed background. Even in my childhood, taverns had NO INDIANS ALLOWED posted. Families kept quiet about Native connections, but gravestones can speak when people cannot. This trip will surprise me.

Pleasant Center Cemetery in Butler County is tucked into a corner of gravel crossroads, catty-corner from a white frame church. Behind a wire fence I find overgrown cedars and uneven rows of stone tablets. This plain churchyard resembles many others within the eighty thousand square miles of Kansas, small islands amid infinite ripples of grass. After marching among rows, I am about to give up when I see the Bruner name, the great-great grandparents' tombstone. It reads: "Charles Jacob Bruner (1833–1912)" and "Mary His Wife (1834–1884)." These words, under floral engraving, is definite proof they existed.

Census records suggest they married sometime after 1850—no marriage license survives. By 1859 they had a son in the household, Francis (later he went by Frank). Their daughter, Lillian, was born in 1866, a dozen years before they arrived in central Kansas.

I examine the tombstone carefully. The handsome stela has unusual embellishment. Above the lettering is a band of entwined scrollwork, with a four-petaled, scalloped blossom at its center. No flower exists in North America with this shape. From beadwork designs I recognize it as the Ojibwa Rose, an Algonquin design. It is also the Medicine Wheel, a representation of stages of life, from birth to old age. The four divisions represent the seasons, from spring to winter, and winds of the four directions.

The tombstone also has the distinctly northeastern Indigenous "double curve" design, which borders the top edge, a marking with many connotations. Although North American people do not have an alphabetic script, they do have a glyphic writing system that goes beyond pictographs. Plains Indian ledger art, two-dimensional war accounts on paper, has a relationship to northeastern Indigenous glyphs. I have studied Cheyenne pictographic writing and published some articles about it. Immediately, I recognize the engravings have meaning beyond ornament.

The double curve, an extended bracket, resembles a canoe that encloses the entire design, in this case inverted to signify death. Indeed, I have seen Algonquin bark carvings of canoes with clan totems within to represent family members. The curvilinear outline also represents the path of the sun from dawn to sunset. On the tombstone elaborate fern tendrils extend the double curve border to fill the spaces. These stems are a type of calendar, as some contemporary beadworkers have told me. Three of the fern fronds are unfurled, representing spring, summer, and fall. The fourth, winter, is curled tightly. Jake never experienced this last season in his death year because he died in November. The fern is coiled, a tiny living spiral never released into this existence.

As I decipher the Bruner stones, I recall my mother showing me two napkins she had appliquéd and embroidered for her hope chest. She used a design from the family Native traditions: mirrored rosebuds, spiral fern tendrils, and ivy. She blended these disparate plants expertly into one flower, a grouping meaningful in terms of glyphs but not botany. The two napkins mirror each other to create a bracket, the Woodland double curve. She learned this embroidery from her Delaware grandmother, long after the exact meanings were lost to her, but the message of the earth's lasting beauty is clear.

When I see the floral patterns on my two-great grandparents' tombstone, I remember my mother teaching me to embroider simple scrolled designs made from satin stitch, running stitch, lover's knot, and chain stitch. I enjoyed the symmetrical, colorful forms taking shape on my tea towels. Mother taught me to love the floral aesthetic, in all its inflections. The garden outside the door was my teacher, as I learned how ferns on the north side of the house were first to green up in the spring. Rosebuds explode into fragrant blooms in full summer. Ivy climbs toward the sky and lasts past frost. The garden outside dies each winter, but the bright floss stitchery does not noticeably fade, nor do etchings on a marble stone.

Most gravestones in the cemetery display Christian symbols—crosses, Bible pages, and the shepherd's crook for lost lambs. What is missing from my grandparents' graves is reference to European

10. Mary Bruner, paternal grandmother of Frank Bruner Junior. Photograph taken in El Dorado, Kansas, between 1878 and 1884. Author's collection. Gift of Gail Bruner Murrow.

religion. This omission speaks loudly. It confirms a family tradition that some family members avoided Christian churches.

On this day of discovery my grandfather has an eerie presence. I imagine how he stood in these same cemetery aisles in 1912, during his grandfather's funeral. Some service took place, whether Native or Christian or both. A cousin sent a copy of Jacob's funeral card, ornamented with feathers, floral designs, and a vague book outline, arced like a double curve more than a Bible.

The practice of transferring Native designs onto tombstones is not well documented, but it occurs in some nearby regional cemeteries. A few people have talked with me about Native designs in tombstone carvings. I have seen a headstone in a small Colorado cemetery with similar Northeast Woodland designs, including an Ojibwa Rose. It had a small grave house built of planks over the site, identical to traditional grave houses on the Menominee reservation today. The similarity between the Colorado gravestone and my grandparents' is remarkable. Later I will find the Bruner design closely resembles Munsee (Stony Country Band) Delaware composition.

This late summer afternoon my husband and I leave tobacco for these grandparents who were almost lost. I am grateful to discover verification of Jake and Mary Bruner's existence as well as the additional narrative added by the floral glyphs, completely unexpected. The Woodland pattern confirms the family Native heritage in another form of Indigenous documentation. In my last glimpse of the cemetery the white-hot sun heats all the stones in a purifying fire. I imagine the peace that will descend once again after we leave.

❖

On a recent visit to Burns my husband and I find the entire downtown is bustling. This is the city's annual Classic Car Show. Model t Fords line up on the brick main street, like they did in Grandfather's lifetime. A man drives one slowly across an intersection, its motor churning like a lawn mower. His feed store cap seems out of place as he steers the elegant old car.

Most of the nineteenth-century downtown is intact. A few antique

11. Frank Bruner Junior on a wagon in Burns, Kansas, with nephew Dan Bruner. Author's collection.

stores flaunt sunflower-trimmed banners and declare they are open for business. Inside the first one I notice peony-trimmed plates on a round oak table, ready for Sunday dinner. Perhaps distant relatives once used them in their kitchens. Colorful quilts hang on walls, similar to the one my great-grandmother Charlotte Bruner made for my mother's wedding day. The pioneer artifacts look no different from those of other small towns. Domestic arts of cooking, gardening, and sewing are universal, whether the women are African American, British Islander, Czech, German, or Native. All brought the same goods from the East.

Grandmother Charlotte's quilt for my mother's hope chest was a circle design, the wedding ring pattern, in pink and white cotton. The interlocking circles resonate with motion of the medicine wheel image. The great number of heirloom quilts in the antique store affirm the widespread practice of this art.

The small town's most numerous businesses are these commercial museums, antique stores where historic castoffs can be restored to the present. The country style of décor is one construed from old-time survival goods such as canning jars. Quilts represent perfect economy—rendering rags into symmetrical, ordered compositions.

As I look around, sun glistens through old bottles, tinted blue from sunlight acting on the glass. Prisms dance in the air, so the room is alive with glistening rays. Only when I look in the back storeroom does the old building seem haunted.

The small town has changed little since my grandfather's boyhood. I find the downtown office where my great-grandfather once presided as a clerk and a postmaster, when the building was new. The brass knob on the door is locked, so I peer through the blurry window and view an empty room, where my grandfather's father must have sat working. I expect to see his face on the other side of the glass as he peers out of the past.

On Main Street ceramic roosters sit by each store, the "roosters on parade" town project. Some are neon orange with white stripes. Others have feathers painted red and brown. They are familiar. My mother displayed a blue ceramic rooster in her kitchen, and I have it to this day. Burns uses the rooster as a community mascot, and like our family, no one explains why. It might hark back to a Spanish rooster pull. This area, near the Santa Fe Trail, was once under Spanish rule. Or a rooster might commemorate poultry as an economic resource. In one family story my grandfather raised fancy breeds of chickens for the county fair, so perhaps it celebrates a countywide specialty.

A parade begins, led by a yellow 1958 Corvette. Little kids run the sidewalks. Dogs bark. Nowhere do I see relatives, only the setting where their lives unfolded. When the last finned Chevrolet rolls past, we look down the street for the last time.

As we leave, my husband sees a figure at the edge of Kickapoo Road, the county throughway named after an Algonquin tribe related to the Delawares. It is a man wearing early-style motorcycle goggles: a ghost or a figment from another time.

"Did your grandfather drive a motorcycle?" he asks.

"Maybe," I say. "He owned a garage for a short time, in 1913. He was mechanical."

I feel a chill but see only grass blowing. Wind is as constant as the passing of time in this rural hamlet. My grandfather's life fades further into the past one more day as sun shinnies down the blue western sky.

❖

In 1889, Grandfather's birth year, all of his family and neighbors struggled through a cycle of hard winters in a hard land. The year before, temperatures had stayed below zero for days. In some isolated farmsteads entire families froze to death. Farming and ranching are hard physical work under the best of circumstances and dangerous. People die from snakebites, falling from horses, and tractor accidents. Weather can kill in any season—drought, tornadoes, floods, lightning, and blizzards.

Perhaps the extreme weather cycle of 1888 brought out the worst in people. Cousins tell me about the rise of prejudice after Grandfather's birth. Vigilante groups such as the Kansas Anti-Horse Thief

12. Frank Bruner Junior as a baby, center, about 1891, with brothers Harry (*left*) and Charles (*right*). Author's collection. Gift of Gail Bruner Murrow.

Association kept rustlers from the lawless Indian Territory, now Oklahoma, from decimating ranches. These groups were independent and often violent. This was frontier country, with justice meted out in beatings and lynchings. After 1900, according to a state survey, lynchings targeted African Americans more often, rather than criminals. That is one visible measure of increasing racism. The Ku Klux Klan began to grow, with some members drawn from the vigilante associations. This was the back story developing when Grandfather was a boy.

During Grandfather's early years, however, all went well enough. My mother told me stories of this time period, when Grandfather was a quiet but stubborn child, sometimes even unruly. He walked to the schoolhouse with his brothers but then slipped out the back door and would be gone all day, wandering the hills. Finally, the teacher sent for his mother. Strong-willed Charlotte forced him to stay. As a boy, Grandfather had an independent streak, but he understood who ran his matriarchal household.

I feel kinship to Grandfather's legacy, from my own long and happy days alone in the countryside. Perhaps, like him, I would have been called "hyperactive." As a child, I spent entire afternoons seeing how fast I could sprint up and down the block. Sitting at a desk was sometimes torturous, even with a hidden book to read, especially in spring, when the air smelled of damp earth. I sympathize with Grandfather's rebellion against school schedules. I never dared to leave the school grounds like he did or face my mother's wrath.

Despite difficult conditions on the Great Plains, trains connected the small town with the outside world. The West of those days had odd mixes of frontier and Victorian cultures. Parlors often had ornate furniture laded in from the East, including pianos, while in the kitchens families subsisted on home-canned tomatoes and eggs. Outhouses were not uncommon in the 1950s and later.

In Grandfather's day trains transported the latest inventions to town, including photography. An uncle by marriage owned a local studio at the turn of the century. His gold-gilt name, Adam Bell, appears at the bottom of a few family portraits. During these years in Burns, the 1890s to 1905, Frank and Charlotte Bruner took their three sons to the photographer regularly. For these occasions they dressed them finely. One portrait shows Grandfather as a baby in a christening gown among Greek columns, a painted backdrop, with his older brothers in Lord Fauntleroy bow ties. Outside the

13. Bruner brothers Charles and Frank Junior, in a deeply shadowed portrait. Photograph taken in Burns, Kansas, area, ca. 1900. Author's collection.

14. Frank Bruner Junior, young boy portrait, taken in Burns, Kansas, area, ca. 1895. Author's collection.

door was the Great Plains, but inside the studio a dream world of European fables took form. Every picture of my grandfather shows him in formal finery.

The offstage presence of Grandfather's parents is almost palpable in the studio photographs—the boys' hair is plastered perfectly into place. Fine jackets, perhaps borrowed from the studio, amplify their small frames. Even in store-bought suits and short hair, the boys' Native origins are apparent. In most images their black hair and brown eyes, as well as darker skin, make striking profiles against sepia paper stock. In a few instances studio tricks lighten their coloring. During development the photographer could "dodge," or overexpose, the negatives and wash out the photograph, although this would leave high-contrast mottling. Several times my grandfather appears to be a blond, but deep shadows in his trousers show the optical trickery. I wonder how that affected Grandfather, who was light-skinned in some photographs and in others wore his own dark skin. Photographs suggest how much of a liability the Native identity was. The photographer had a repertoire of disguises, and he used them. The dodged photographs added to a family narrative of European ancestry.

The Root and Bruner families presented themselves as European Americans and participants in American society, not Indians. As Americans, they could vote and maintain households independently, unlike Native people on reservations. They could be citizens. An 1871 law made "Indians" wards of the government. Native children could be removed and forced to attend distant boarding schools with Christian sponsors. Indian agents maintained control of any financial assets. My family chose to suppress their Native heritage so they could keep their children. They kept their families intact, without knowing that the process of self-denial would have long-range ripples. Erasure of identity has costs, but survival trumps everything else.

❖

Something happened to Grandfather's family as the twentieth century began. Perhaps it was a series of small incidents or one catastrophic event. The Ku Klux Klan became a major threat. Community members burned people in effigy as late as the 1960s. Sometimes my grandfather gave me short homilies during card games. Looking back, I see how he staged conversations deliberately as we played casino and gin rummy. Grandfather paced his speech as he told stories, so the images imprinted deeply. My most vivid memories of my grandfather are conversations about persecution, through tarring and feathering. Tar in those days was tree sap, not asphalt, but still the process was painful and humiliating.

One day after school, when I was about ten years old, we sat down at a sunny table. He shuffled, dealt, but did not pick up his hand. I held my cards and waited. "Ku Klux Klan men are such cowards, they have to gang up on one man," he said. "They don't fight a fair fight."

"Who are they?" I asked, as this was no part of my young life experience. He went on to describe masked men who rode horses through the countryside. He paused to give me time to imagine horses and Halloween sheet costumes. "Once they caught a man and rolled him in hot pine tar," he said and stopped to inhale his cigarette. "Then they rolled him in stinking chicken feathers." Smoke lingered over the table another beat. He had my attention. "With chicken droppings. That's what they call 'tar and feathering.'" I thought about how this would hurt and stink. "They ran him through the middle of town naked. You don't recover all the way after that." He picked up the cards, and we continued the game, without our usual patter. That horrible image settled in my mind.

Years later I understand he was telling more than an isolated anecdote. He was explaining his own life, the threats he had experienced directly, as "the man" targeted by the KKK. Perhaps he also described his own humiliation as explanation for his unsettled wanderings. He had reason to escape this harsh reality, through travel or through alcohol.

African Americans, Catholics, and Mexican Americans all were targets of the KKK in that region of Kansas. A cousin told me how townspeople spread disparaging gossip that Grandfather and his brothers were Mexican. That rumor persisted for years. In the mid-plains region most Mexicans are descended from Native populations, not European Spaniards, so this was not far removed from the truth. The KKK is a common enemy. Kansas was the first state to declare the Klan unconstitutional, in 1925, after decades of its existence. But the law did not change hearts of forty thousand Klan members overnight. The vigilante threat was very real in Grandfather's day, both before and after 1925.

This firsthand story from Grandfather opened my eyes to a world beyond the Disney characters on the neighbor's television. When I went to school the next day, I felt removed from my classmates as I pondered Grandfather's tale. Neighbors could be friends one moment and turn into a punishing mob the next. Since my grandfather was different, I also had a double identity. On the way home I ran past alleys and felt safe only when I reached my own yard.

Another time, after a card game ended, Grandfather talked directly about the importance of fighting the KKK. "In secret meetings," he said, "I spoke against them, said they had no place in town." He found enough like-minded people to stand with him. "We let them know they had to go." From Grandfather I learned the existence of a mob whose members tar and feather victims and who threaten violence against outnumbered victims.

The Ku Klux Klan created bitter divisions among families. Some of my father's wealthy relatives attended KKK meetings, not to protest but to participate, including my other grandfather. I imagine both of my grandfathers at a Klan meeting, on opposite sides. The distance between the two families could not have been any greater. The tensions my sister Mary remembered were deeper than she knew.

Grandfather's stories made it clear that speaking up is important as well as taking a stand. Words can transform victims into effective fighters. In my child's eyes Grandfather was indeed a hero. I hoped one day I would be able to speak like him. Placement of words and their timing were critical as he relayed his stories. I was spellbound.

The rise of the KKK explains, in part, the dispersal of Grandfather's family, including his parents and brother. Even though the Bair, Bruner, and Root families had homesteaded the land around Burns, most left by 1905. The Root brothers scattered to California, New Mexico, Oregon, and larger Kansas towns.

Grandfather's parents relocated to a Kansas City neighborhood of Native people, on former Delaware holdings. There they were beyond the reach of the KKK marauders. Frank Senior appears in city directories as a foreman in a Kansas City warehouse. In the census records the sons attend school, and then, by the next census, they work as clerks. Years pass, and city directories record their continuing residence and occupations, in a place far from Burns.

Grandfather's family presence in his hometown is negligible. A few photographs remain and a few mentions in town annals. Still, this was home, where everyone reconvened in later years. Brother Harry repurchased the Samuel Root homestead in 1929. The parents—Frank Senior and Charlotte—returned to live with their banker son, Charles, in the 1940s until they died. As a married man, my grandfather found employment in a nearby town, Newton, and lived there, not Kansas City, most of his adulthood. All are buried together in the countryside around Burns, most under tombstones etched with floral designs.

After his nearly seventy years of life, Grandfather rests. Under the cathedral of sky he is again a brother, son, nephew, grandson, and great-grandson. As far as I travel, I only feel at home near them, in the Flint Hills, where sky reaches closer to the stars than anywhere else. In this eternity everyone is beyond all threats.

❖

Kansas City is the place where my mother remembered visiting her Bruner grandparents, not the central Kansas grasslands. She grew up in Newton, near Burns, on the Chisholm Trail. Ties to the dispersed family in Kansas City remained strong. She rode the train to visit and sometimes for extended stays throughout the 1920s and 1930s. She told me bits and pieces about this family time period, in no particular order, and they illuminate parts of her father's life. He lived as a Native man unmoored from reservation life yet not assimilated into another social order. In Kansas City he and his parents found others in the same limbo.

"Citizen Delawares" of Kansas, as those not affiliated with the Oklahoma tribe were called, continued to live near each other in former Delaware communities, alongside Wyandots. They lived as Delawares always have lived, along creeks and rivers. Northeastern Kansas is a glaciated topography of bluffs like much of the eastern woodlands. Even today, the downtown has intervals of tree-lined streams interrupting the traffic ways. Across the river Kansas City, Missouri's skyline rises over expanses of urban, concrete structures. It contrasts with the Kansas side, where a block from downtown, gardens are common. People still fish the rivers commercially. A few years ago a friend took me to a Kansas City market where local turtles, gar, crayfish, and perch are for sale. Trapping on the river may still continue. I remember Lawrence beaver trappers in the 1960s providing meat for downtown bars. Hunting seasons for deer, wild turkey, geese, sandhill cranes, and many other types of game are under the state's jurisdiction. In Grandfather's day people could supplement subsistence living by working at meatpacking plants, rail yards, and warehouses. In Kansas City no one went hungry.

Grandfather's parents lived at 551 Freeman Avenue, near Jersey Creek and the early Delaware "pay house," or government agent's building. Wyandot tribal members John Armstrong, Charles Garrett, and William Walker all had homes in that neighborhood, just before Grandfather's parents lived there. Today the hereditary chief of the Kansas Wyandots is Janith English, and I have heard her pray in her language. The Kansas Wyandot and Delaware communities are barely visible to outsiders, but they maintain regular tribal events. The Wyandotte Nation of Oklahoma has reasserted its claim to downtown Kansas City lands. In 2008 it opened the 7th Street Casino, a few blocks away from Grandfather's house on Freeman Street.

During my mother's childhood she did not notice differences

between her Miller grandparents of Irish and German heritage and her Bruner and Root grandparents. According to her, differences were just family peculiarities. Mother repeated brief parables about her father—disjointed, but each had a moral lesson.

One summer afternoon when I visited her, she took a drink of ice tea and set it down. "During the Depression," she said, "Grandfather sold off the land. One of the sons got the farm, one bought into the bank, and my father became a pharmacist." This was her ritualized tale about the family migration to Kansas City. Each sibling has a place. Like a fairy tale, though, the youngest son of three is the special one.

"Yes, Mama," I said. Agreement was easier, even if I knew the timeline was jumbled. Her family stories were true, just mixed-up. Census records indicate the family moved in 1905, not the 1930s Great Depression. Perhaps another mild recession of 1902 to 1904 was part of her family's experience, and she conflated it with the 1930s time period. One brother did stay with the bank, but he worked under Samuel Cobb until 1909. The family land changed hands in the early 1900s. She finished her tea and was done. This was typical of how she told family stories. She had shorthand accounts, not epics.

The third brother, my grandfather, was sixteen when the Bruner family moved to Kansas City, still a student. My mother explained another time: "Father graduated from Wyandotte High School. He took Latin, so he would know medical terms for a career as a pharmacist." She went on to tell how he was a top student, slow but thorough. "He insisted I take four years of German, not just two and then switch to French. He thought a person should learn one language well."

When I researched Grandfather's experiences as a young man, I found he never was a pharmacist, but in the 1910 United States census, at age twenty-one, he appears as a drugstore clerk in Norton, Kansas, near the Penokee Man image. He worked for a druggist named George Moulton. Moulton's establishment sold tobacco, laudanum, slippery elm bark, licorice, and cinnamon drops.

Moulton also had a criminal record. The state convicted him

for selling "rock and rye" without an alcohol permit, just a few years before Grandfather arrived in Norton. The case went to the Kansas Supreme Court, so it must have been a well-known, if not serious, transgression.

My grandfather may have learned the shady past of Moulton and left this position, or perhaps he could not adjust to the incessant western wind. He survived this remote town for only a short time. Within weeks he appears in another 1910 census, counted twice, and again listed as a drugstore clerk, this time in Kansas City. As a young man, he clerked in pharmacies, perhaps as an apprentice in training for certification from the state board. He never attained this vocation. This absence of achievement is the negative image of a story, one never passed on.

When she was a very small child, not long after her 1915 birth, Mother remembers these early years. Grandfather worked in a pharmacy with regular refrigeration, rare in those days. When he came home, he brought ice cream for the family, a luxury. He doted on his small daughter and insisted that she be awakened for this treat. It was one of her best childhood memories. Without explanation, though, he changed direction and never returned to this field of employment. It is but one of many interruptions in his work life.

❖

On overcast, cold days I feel close to my grandfather. I discern his plaid flannel shirt and plain trousers. Then his face takes form. His cheeks are concave hollows below his cheekbones, and his whiskers, though shaven, make his skin grizzled. How difficult it is to imagine this old man as a talented young athlete. Yet in Kansas City, before his marriage in 1914, he played professional baseball for several teams, including the Kansas City Blues.

Athletic ability ran in the family. His older brother, Harry Bruner, had been a star on a Young Men's Christian Association baseball team, so Grandfather followed that example and also excelled. This was the era when basketball evolved into a national sport. One family story tells how Uncle Harry broke Forrest Clare "Phog"

Allen's nose during a game. Allen, protégé of the game's inventor, James Naismith, went on to develop basketball beyond the peach basket hoop phase as a coach at the University of Kansas and also Haskell Institute, the Indian boarding school in Lawrence.

Uncle Harry also was a first-rate runner and held a national indoor track sprint record documented in the Kansas City newspapers. Grandfather did not leave such a record of sports achievements. He probably participated in basketball and track, but baseball was his chosen sport. He told stories about his athletic feats to his family.

The most substantial evidence of Grandfather's baseball career was his gnarled hands. Grandfather played the physically demanding position of catcher before padded mitts were standard equipment. Several times fastballs broke his fingers, which in old age were knotted with arthritis. The life of a professional baseball player was tough in the early 1900s. Grandfather told my brother about traveling with the Blues from one small town to the next by train. The Kansas City Public Library has records of the Blues, exactly as Grandfather remembered, but only with accounts of wins and losses, not rosters. Baseball was poorly documented during this era, and players were as transient as the poorly organized teams.

In the early years of the 1900s, in his late teens and early twenties, Grandfather put on the simple uniform with the Kansas City Blues logo appliquéd in royal blue. He took to the field and must have had a passion for the stick-and-ball game developed from both European and Native traditions. In the wide expanses of the Midwest, sports connect towns with each other. They create dramatic scenarios each time a pitcher winds up and challenges a batter. These small duels, less literary than Greek dramas, nonetheless fulfill some cathartic role in communities. Some of my own earliest memories, from the late 1940s into the 1950s, are voices of sports announcers, mixing with the rasp of cicadas in the hot summer nights. Each traveled through the air into our stuffy house, a balance of natural and human voices.

This must have been a wonderful time for my grandfather as he

15. Eva, or Evelyn, Miller in Kansas City, Kansas, early twentieth century. She married Frank Bruner Junior in 1914 or 1915. Author's collection.

mastered a sport and played at a professional level. Finally, Grand-father chose family life over traveling with the team, he told my brother, so he resigned. But time moved forward. He may have been good enough to play on a better-known team, but he chose to leave the unsettled lifestyle best suited for single individuals. As his descendant, I have to be grateful for the decision that led to my existence.

Grandchildren meet their grandparents at the end, as fallen heroes facing mortality. We remember their decline and deaths. None of us alive today saw Grandfather's best years as a young ballplayer in Kansas City.

❖

Grandfather hunted. He knew how to shoot and dress game for family meals, and family was the center of his life. As an older man, he raised poultry and rabbits for the table as a regular source of meat. I think of this, the responsibility for being a family's provider, while driving to the cemetery where he rests in the Flint Hills of Kansas. Overhead two large birds circle high against clouds. They look like eagle mates. Hundreds of mice rustle through the grasses around me, and these will be good meals for the raptors.

On this trip to the graveside in Florence, Kansas, I carry cigarettes and a shot of whiskey for Grandfather. These tokens of earthly life smell strong on the breeze. The herb tobacco, sometimes mixed with red willow and sumac, is *kinnikinnik*, a smoking mixture. Its smoke wafts beyond sight, so prayers can rise to the heavens. Whiskey's biting smell, as it evaporates, also penetrates to the other world. For my grandmother, who liked geraniums, I bring a handful of the clarion red blossoms to place on her tombstone. They sweeten the afterworld's dank soil. The two lie alongside each other after their long marriage, still companions.

She may have met him in high school or afterward, when she clerked at Macy's in Kansas City, about 1913. My mother kept a photograph of Grandmother from those days, chic in a princess style coat and matching hat. As a young, single woman, she worked long hours but found time to primp. He must have caught her eye: a dark, slender man with movie star good looks, and he knew how to dress. Even as a boy, photographs show him in snappy formal suits. Their courtship is forgotten, and no story remains about how the two families accepted each other. No marriage license exists. Interracial marriage was illegal in Missouri until 1967, but Kansas never had miscegenation laws from the time of its formation as a state. Probably the couple married in Kansas City, Kansas, where both their parents lived.

Some hand-tatted lace is among my mother's mementos, and it could have been hers. Later the lace was on my sister Jane's wedding dress. Grandmother's engagement ring has a beautiful filigree gold setting, lacy also—but with a glass stone. My mother claimed a jeweler switched the stones, but I suspect the real diamond was bartered for cash. After years of just getting by, no luxury remained.

My sister Mary told me Grandmother and Grandfather had some good years together, among the many hardships. I can only imagine Grandmother's feelings when in his later years Grandfather disappeared on open-ended journeys. She always waited at home. In those days women most often stayed in marriages, but Grandmother could have left. She had experience working as a young woman and also she had family. She chose not to leave.

Their grandchildren have scattered from the East to the West Coasts. I am the only descendant left in Kansas, and I miss my siblings and cousins. Overhead, as the two eagles loop away from each other and then return, I feel less alone. Eagles once were rare in this part of the country, and their silhouettes still create a hush. These are golden eagles, feathered angels of the Great Plains with tawny brown markings. It is a warm day, not the frigid weather when they occasionally ride cold wind riptides over the northern prairies, so these two must be yearlong residents. When I notice the first one, the larger female, she might be my own confabulation. The second one, then, stills my doubts. As they continue to circle, I call to them. They also are Grandmother and Grandfather. In the absence of my grandparents through most of my life, I look to the land to present kinship in the natural world. They are comfort in the cold wind.

I swallow a sip of whiskey myself, exhale a last breath of cigarette smoke, and leave fresh tobacco by the headstone. I thank all the family for their hard lives—Grandmother, Grandfather, and my mother, whose ashes are buried with them. I remember their twin baby daughters who also lie, unmarked, in this plot. Finally, I thank the eagles for their presence.

The graves face the western horizon, where earth and sky create a jagged line of blue vapor. In summer mirages appear in that distance, moisture shimmering against waves of yellow hay. When sun descends into its own fire, light evaporates from engraved letters of Grandmother's and Grandfather's names. So my grandparents, together, face west for eternity. Their courtship story is lost, yet the results remain. In the sequence of generations they passed forward the gift of life.

❖

Grandfather did not participate in the military during World War I. He once told me he was too young for the first war of his youth, the Spanish-American War, and too old for World War I. His 1917 draft card shows he was twenty-seven years old when "C. W. Stratford, registrar," signed his exemption form.

When he talked to me once about missing the armed service, his voice had a timbre of regret. "I wanted to fight," he said. "I was no coward." He wanted to fulfill a man's responsibility, but he was exempted from the war because he had a wife and child. He had started a business, which he would lose if he left, and his family had no other means of support.

Grandfather's World War I registration card shows he owned Butler County Garage, an early car repair enterprise. Uncle's wife, Theress (McCann) Bruner, remembers her father-in-law owned this business in El Dorado, a few miles from Burns, Kansas. He was, however, "too soft-hearted" to collect debts, she told me, so the business went broke. With the Ku Klux Klan in the vicinity,

this may have cut down on his clientele as well. That is the only
business he ever owned.

I wonder how much his "Indian"-looking appearance limited
his work choices. For most of his adult life he worked as a laborer,
often at dangerous jobs. During World War I my mother remembers
living in Oakland, California, briefly, while Grandfather worked on
the docks, demanding physical work. She was three years old and
barely remembered the bay, a great change from the grasslands.
This work allowed him to contribute his labor to support the war
effort while still sustaining his family.

Later, by 1918, the small family returned to Kansas City. My
mother often talked about Grandfather's next job, endless days in a
meatpacking plant. Sinclair Lewis would write about the hardships
of this kind of work. Grandfather never allowed the family to eat hot
dogs after he saw what offal went into them. This was employment
of last resort. Conditions were harsh, with long shifts, no unions,
no medical assistance, and no recourse when injuries occurred.

Grandfather became involved in the fight to establish unions. He
told me about this struggle during his history lesson card games.
One winter afternoon during Christmas holidays, he dealt, arranged
his cards as usual, and waited. I sorted highest cards to the left
and then realized he was about to speak. He cleared his throat and
said, "Unions did not always exist." This gave me pause. My father
was a union representative, and the phone rang often. I did not
understand all the talk, but I knew it was important. I waited for
my grandfather to continue.

"Men met in secret at night because they feared the company
men would beat them to death." I thought about this a moment,
startled. Who would want to kill my grandfather? He continued:
"We wore sacks over our heads—flour sacks with eyes cut out. That
way the informants could not take our names back to the bosses."

I could hardly believe he had experienced this hardship or that
people could be so cruel. This was not a history I was learning at
school. "If men lost their fingers or arms in the machinery," he

said, "they were fired. If they fell asleep after long hours, they were fired." He paused, then gathered the cards and dealt another hand.

I said nothing, but I watched him closely to make sure he was finished before I turned back to my cards. His descriptions of mutilations frightened me. I was a child, but I knew this was an important story, and I always remembered it. My brother told me later that Grandfather used obscenity to describe how Kansas had passed anti-union laws, the "right-to-work" laws, in 1958.

Other relatives treated me as an inconsequential female who should learn charm and domestic skills. Grandfather honored me, a young girl, with important knowledge. He practiced feminism years before the term had become well known. He showed how I had importance outside the household. I needed to learn how to stand up against bullies.

Grandfather was a lifelong Democrat, despite the Lincoln Republican majority around him, because of the party's policies to protect the working class. "Once," he said during another card game, "a lifelong friend ran for a city office. But he was a Republican. I planned to vote for him, but when I got to the polling booth," he laughed at his own stubborn nature, "I just couldn't do it." He voted the straight Democrat ticket to support worker ideology.

My mother told me how Grandfather believed no man was worth a million dollars. No labor any man did could merit that extreme income, he explained to her. He never made anywhere close to a million dollars. Grandfather struggled to find a place for himself in the economic system. From his marriage in 1914 until the 1920s, he worked many jobs. He lost them or quit or moved on. He also suffered the tragic loss of two children, which scarred him and his wife. Throughout all these years he did not give up his principles.

❖

Late in my mother's life, long after her father's death, I discovered family photographs in her basement. I took the fragile scrapbook of black pages to my mother. She turned the soft paper slowly as we reviewed her baby pictures.

"Oh," she said suddenly and then sat stricken. "That is my sister who died."

I looked at the photograph of a round-faced baby, a stranger to me. Mother said, "Photographs should always have names on the back and dates," and she handed me back the photographs. "This is Mary Jane."

As my mother remained lost in thought, I penciled in the name of this lost baby. The silence deepened as I etched lead across paper.

"She was born in 1921," she finally added. I wrote the date for posterity.

Then she told the story. Her twin sisters were born between her and her brother. One died at birth. Delivery of twins was hazardous to the mother and the babies, so the loss of one infant was not uncommon. It was not tragic. But the living one, the one in this photograph, lived only a few years. She became sickly for a long time and then died. After a moment of silence Mother continued: "In those days doctors lost many children because their knowledge was limited. Besides that, my parents were poor."

We both understood what that meant—they could not afford every option for the sick child. "After the second baby died," my mother said, "my parents were never the same."

This conversation was the first I knew of these small aunts who had existed so briefly. The sepia cardboard of Mary Jane's image was badly faded, but I could see white organdy and lace festooning the smiling infant. She was clearly beloved.

My mother would never speak of this again. My mother was six years old in 1921. Death of the newborn might have been hidden from her, but loss of the toddler would have loomed large in the mind of a little girl who played with dolls and helped with a new baby. Her lifelong anxieties may have been related to this loss. As an adult, my mother named her first daughter Mary and her second daughter Jane, and so the lost child's name continued.

After this conversation I better understood why my grandmother always seemed on the verge of tears. I remember her in our living room, sitting uneasily on the edge of her suitcase, ready for a train two hours before departure. Her anxiety was palpable. I also understood the hollows under my grandfather's eyes. Sorrow is an undertow in our family's conversation. We remember startling calls in the night with the worst possible news.

One night when I was a teenager, the phone rang at three o'clock in the morning. My father got out of bed and answered, and then I heard my mother wailing. My sister Mary's first child had died of pneumonia. The terror of that jangling nighttime call stays with me.

Other Delaware descendants live in the Kansas region, and as we exchange stories, lost children is a recurring theme. Gretchen Eick, a Wichita friend, told me her story of her colonial Delaware grandmother losing two children in Pennsylvania. A Dutch couple had only one grown son, who was very sickly, probably with tuberculosis. Delaware people traveled through the Dutch community on hunting trips, and so the parents of the frail young man decided on a plan. They became friendly with the Delawares. The found a healthy Delaware woman who agreed to marry their son. In time she bore two children. When the son died, however, the grandparents took the children for their own and forced the mother to leave. That Delaware woman sued the court to retrieve her children, and her letters are a record of the conflict. She lost, but generations of grandchildren remember the cruel loss for that grandmother. They pass down the court documents to ensure no one in the family forgets.

A 1782 mob killing of ninety Delaware men, women, and children in Gnadenhutten, Ohio, is another story of tragedies from past centuries. The Christianized Delawares were slaughtered and scalped after time for hymns and prayers. Murders of the children were especially brutal.

As I grew up, I was made aware that everything could suddenly change forever, as when a tornado struck or unpredictable illnesses ended people's lives. Or violence. When my mother babysat my children, she held them closely, as though they could be taken away at any moment. She participated in a sad tradition of loss.

Throughout the first years of marriage, Grandfather attempted many jobs. He started at a good job in Concordia, as a hay inspector, but within days of the family's arrival, a tornado struck. This terrified my grandmother, who was a city girl and not used to the Great Plains weather. She insisted that they move. Grandfather listened to his wife and complied. Respect for a woman's opinion is woven into family stories through the generations.

Finally, in 1923, Grandfather started a job with the Atchison, Topeka & Santa Fe Railway. Grandmother and Grandfather resettled in Newton, a town less than thirty miles from his birthplace. His new and dangerous job as a switchman required strength and foolhardiness. Duties included riding atop cars, setting breaks, connecting air hoses to cars, and all details of switching cars from one train to another. He worked at this job almost twenty years.

The railroad position was the cornerstone of family prosperity. After a few years they were able to move into a respectable bungalow. Grandfather and Grandmother welcomed a healthy son, Robert Lathrop, into their family. He was eight years younger than my mother.

These were the most settled years of my mother's childhood. She was a beauty, and she did well in school. Both of my grandparents were proud of their firstborn daughter, and the new baby had no problems. The American dream was working, for a golden moment. If only the story could end at this moment, at 219 Oak Street, Newton, Kansas.

❖

More stories about Grandfather's Kansas City years come from the 1920s. When my mother was about ten, her little brother became ill, and to avoid contagion, her parents sent her to Kansas City. My mother stayed an entire school term with her Bruner grandparents. When she remembered her Bruner grandparents, this was the setting.

A Native strategy to survive pestilence was to break the family into smaller groups and scatter. In the crisis of illness the extended family provides a safety net. My grandfather sent his precious oldest child to live with his parents, rather than risk her death. Few stories remain from his young adulthood, but his actions show he was careful. He was close to his parents and called on them to care for his firstborn.

Great-Grandmother Charlotte ran the Kansas City household, and everyone obeyed her. My mother remembered how unusual she was, especially compared to women of European descent in Newton, on the Kansas plains. Grandmother Charlotte refused to go to church. She could be a good person, she told her granddaughter, without being Christian. My mother always explained this with pride, even though she herself identified as an Episcopalian. Charlotte did not directly teach my mother Delaware religion, but she taught daily values. Hospitality was an important virtue as well as generosity. Grandmother kept a pot of stew simmering on the stove all day, so anyone could eat when hungry. Hoboes learned to find Grandmother's house, where she provided each a bowl of food. Charlotte was a capable woman—tall and sturdy. She had a hunting rifle handy and never had any trouble with the more desperate men. She knew how to shoot and defend her home.

My mother remembered how Grandmother Charlotte worked hard in a large garden. Asparagus creamed with hard-boiled eggs from the hens was a favorite meal. The backyard plot produced snap beans, corn, squash, peas, peppers, potatoes, and tomatoes. All of this was in the middle of Kansas City, but it was not unlike the farm. Her husband and sons no doubt helped with heavy work, under her direction, as my father tilled our garden in the springtime.

My mother returned home to Newton after her brother recovered fully. She visited Kansas City other times, but this long-term visit is the one most vividly recorded in her childhood memories. Grandfather Bruner received the *Kansas City Star* each day, read it, and worked the crossword puzzles. He taught her how to read the paper, starting with the headlines. He had patience as this busy granddaughter tussled with the pages and sounded out words. My mother remembered her grandparents with great affection.

The marriage between Charlotte and Frank Bruner Senior was not without incident. A cousin tells one story: The old man tried to sneak through a window after a night of carousing. Grandmother Charlotte knocked him unconscious with an iron skillet. Misuse of alcohol is an obvious part of the story, along with the woman's righteous anger. Was this an isolated happening, or was it a conflation of many times when this happened? Details are lost, but the example of women's strength is clear. The husband feared his wife's wrath, with good reason. No stories of wife beatings are part of the family legends.

Grandfather's parents lived in Kansas City from 1905 until World War II started. By then they were elderly. They returned to live in Burns with the most prosperous son, the banker. Frank Senior died first, in 1941, and Charlotte lived until 1954.

During her years as a widow, Grandmother Charlotte cut a dramatic figure in Burns. She wore a coat outside, no matter how hot the weather was. She pestered her banker son by charging goods downtown and leaving him to pay. She would order "beer" at the pharmacy, and when given root beer, she crowed about it, causing a commotion. She always carried a derringer. She teased her Burns area grandchildren with it—almost allowing them to touch the miniature firearm but then pulling it away at the last minute. I wonder if the derringer still fires, if it fits into a cousin's handbag among lace handkerchiefs.

During these last years often my grandfather visited his parents in Burns for Sunday dinner. Uncle Bob told me about these excursions into the countryside until, abruptly, the visits ended. The sudden break occurred with no explanation, the recurring theme from the days of Jake Bruner and before. Perhaps, simply, Grandmother Charlotte died, and she was the one who had held them together. That was the last my uncle remembered seeing that part of his family with any regularity.

Charlotte and Frank Senior lie buried together in the Burns cemetery, their stories suspended but not concluded. They cared for my mother during the family crisis and supported their son, my grandfather, as he struggled to keep his children alive. The time my mother spent with Grandmother Charlotte and Grandfather Frank,

16. Robert Lathrop Bruner (1923–2013), son of Frank Bruner Junior and Eva (Miller) Bruner. Photograph taken in Newton, Kansas, about 1940. Author's collection.

her Delaware grandparents, was memorable for her. We are made up of many fractions of bloodlines, but family inheritance is not a single pattern so easily measured by mathematic abstractions. My mother's time with the Bruner side of her family influenced her greatly during impressionable years.

❖

Uncle, born in 1923, remembered that when his mother was mad at her husband, she blamed his "Indian blood." So that was the family oral tradition: Indian blood dwells within us as a dark shadow that can arise at any time and cause trouble. I have heard other people say they have bad tempers because of their Indian blood, or they are stubborn or stoic or reticent or alcoholic. The stereotypes continue, but at least when his Irish and German American mother was angry, Uncle learned his father's identity, even if it was a negative epithet. This cursing was after calamity ended the good years of the family. It was after a random accident at work.

Indian blood has been the rationale for Grandfather's drinking in his later years, but my older brother gives me another perspective. I visit him and his wife in northern Arizona, where he lives within rings of volcanic mountains.

He greets me outside, and while he parks the car, his dogs sniff me over thoroughly. After the dogs celebrate my entrance, he seats me at his dining room table. It is round, almost identical to my older sister's, and our conversations are similar. He also spent extended time with our grandparents. After he attended Harvard, at age seventeen, he stayed out a year and worked at a Kansas newspaper before returning to complete his degree. The newspaper was in Hutchinson, a few miles from Newton, where our grandparents and Uncle Bob lived. He learned firsthand stories from our grandfather.

"Perhaps you would like red wine," he says to me. Dogs and wine are comforting family rituals.

The open bottle is on the table, aerating. We settle and sip a rich Malbec. After sharing news, I ask, "Please tell me again about Pop's injury. When did it happen?"

17. Frank Bruner Junior and grandson David Dotson, ca. 1958. Photograph taken at Emporia, Kansas. Author's collection.

"I don't know exact dates."

Talking to my brother is odd because I copy so many of his gestures. I followed him around when I was a toddler and imitated him as closely as possible. He twists his mouth sideways while contemplating a slightly unpleasant idea, as I might.

I try to jog Brother's memory, "He worked for the Santa Fe railroad in Newton for twenty years. He must not have stayed with the railroad long after that."

"No," my brother agrees. "He received disability, a small sum but enough to get by. He was drawing disability when I visited him, about 1961, when I was working for the newspaper. He was old then—it was a few years before he died." My brother goes on to recount this life-changing tragedy of Grandfather's work life. Grandfather, then in his fifties, was switching cars among trains in the railroad yards. Suddenly, a load in a boxcar shifted and slammed him in the head. He never recovered fully. The accident changed the fortunes of the family.

This was after my mother had married, so the family downsized and moved to a smaller house. Uncle Bob was still a boy, and he worked odd jobs as soon as he was able.

My brother stops a moment, then says, "Use of alcohol probably became habitual for Pop, especially with Prohibition over. Alcohol laced with laudanum was a regular pain relieving medicine in the pharmacies. What else could he do?"

I think about those tough times and say, "Yes, who can blame him?" My other grandmother bragged how she had taken the pledge to never drink but took brandy for "female trouble" each month as medicine. Medicinal brandy was in a separate category from saloon whiskey. "Pop knew what was available in pharmacies, with his background working in them."

I think back to my visit with our uncle a few years earlier. I tell my brother: "Uncle Bob told me how he grew up in a small house near the edge of Newton, but with a lot big enough for a garden. It is right next to Sand Creek, so soil would be good." I pause and count years. "That would be the late 1930s because Uncle Bob was born in 1923." I recall how I drove by the house the summer before, and it was smaller than I had imagined. "The yard was just big enough for a garden. Uncle Bob said Grandfather stacked rabbit cages across the back and raised them for meat. Cinnamon lop ears, other fancy breeds." That part of Kansas continues to be a commercial source for rabbit meat. "When you visit Kansas, I'll take you by the Rare Hare farm out by El Dorado," I say. "You can find rabbit meat regularly in the restaurants. I always wonder if they descend from the lineage Grandfather raised." We both laugh.

"I don't remember that house," says my brother. "They were

living in a small apartment downtown when I knew them. They were terribly poor."

"Uncle Bob said they built a coop and had chickens, pigeons, and guinea hens," I say. "When he was a boy, they always entered poultry in the fair and won medals as well as some cash. Several times he went to the state fair in Hutchinson with his winning entries."

"I never knew that," says my brother.

The truck farming years were long over when my brother visited in the 1960s. We both agree that Grandfather found ways to survive with his disability. He raised his teenaged son, and he also befriended our father's younger brother, Robert Dotson, who was the same age as his son. My father told me how Grandfather Bruner had influenced Robert and other people, in quiet ways. Robert liked being around the garden and learned agricultural skills. Grandfather Bruner had helped shape this young in-law greatly—Robert later studied agronomy in college and became a professor in that field.

"Pop was always good with children," says David.

"Yes, I remember," I say. "He played cards with me for hours and talked to me like I was a person, not just a fluff girl. He never condescended." He modeled to me how children are active beings capable of dialogue, not the blank slate idea of childhood that was current in the 1950s. This modest man demonstrated by example rather than by issuing orders to his underlings. Most details of my grandfather's existence within the community of Newton have vanished, but his legacy remains through his influence on his son, son-in-law, grandson, and also the brother of his son-in-law.

American Indians of Grandfather's generation had limited acceptance in small towns like Newton. My mother talked about the Oklahoma Native man Frank Lindley, who was the revered basketball coach of her high school from 1914 to 1945 and also its principal. "Chief," as he was called, devoted himself to school athletes, many of whom went to the University of Kansas to play under James Naismith. He authored books about basketball and invented the zone defense. But when, after many years, he applied for school superintendent, he was turned down. So he resigned and left town.

Invisible lines of bias create complex social rules in isolated prairie towns, as Lindley discovered. My grandfather, with his Indian blood, also could not fully participate in community life, especially with his burden of chronic pain.

"Did Pop ever talk about being Indian?" I ask my brother.

"Never," he says. "It was just understood."

"Uncle Bob doesn't remember ever talking to his dad about it," I say. "Perhaps he took a vow."

"It would be a real barrier in the small town," says my brother. "Letting it go was a reasonable choice under the circumstances."

We agree our grandfather made an unspoken decision to never discuss his background. He chose his wife's people. For Delaware and other related groups, children follow the mother's traditions. A man expected the woman's family to take precedence.

Our German Irish grandmother gave her children a foothold in the mostly white community. Blood, however, does not follow human direction. Even our grandmother would make occasional comments about the Native lineage that also imprinted our family. *Indian blood* was her stereotyped term for problems that Irish, Germans, and just about everyone else might have.

California was a place Grandfather visited as a young man, where some of his Root cousins had settled. Grandfather knew how to hop a train and ride the rails, so he might have traveled the West Coast widely before marriage. In his later years, my brother told me, our grandfather meandered away from his Kansas home and ended up in distant states. Grandmother would receive a call in the night, or Uncle Bob would. Maybe Pop was on binges. Maybe he needed to get out of the small town's isolation. No one ever knew the full story, but always Grandfather found his way back.

On our visit my brother told me about the disastrous poker game that occurred in the 1940s, a night of terrible losses. At this time my grandfather suffered aftereffects of his head injury, maybe complicated by drinking. Perhaps his employers were involved.

18. Frank Bruner Junior and Evelyn (Miller) Bruner in Oakland, 1940s. Author's collection.

"Grandfather was set up to lose," my brother explained. "He gambled big on a sure hand. Four aces, odds of one in fifty thousand draws." My brother himself is a skilled cardplayer, and he memorized all the odds while a teenager. "But his opponent," my brother continued, "had a straight flush, clubs." This coincidence was incomprehensible, and Brother made it clear cheating was involved. If it were railroad men who swindled our grandfather, which fits with dates of his work record, then this was one way he could be removed from the payroll without legal difficulties. A disabled worker was a liability.

"No one knows the full story," my brother concluded.

Whatever the ultimate cause, this incident resulted in complete financial bankruptcy. Grandfather lost all his savings—probably the house, plus more. This was a time of great difficulties. Grandfather's own father had died, so he was grieving. Grandfather was in his early fifties, injured, and unable to work as a laborer.

Grandfather and Grandmother made a new life in Oakland, California, where Grandmother worked at a department store for a regular salary. My oldest sister remembered that our grandmother was in the women's clothing department. She was the family breadwinner—almost unheard of in the late 1940s. Widows and wives of service men worked but not women in households with men. This job was an opportunity, a position she would never have in her Kansas hometown. She started paying into her own social security fund.

My brother remembers how fond both Grandfather and Grandmother had been of Oakland. They lived near a park, and a group of men had a regular poker game. I suspect Grandfather was the ace player and won often.

One afternoon, Grandfather dressed in a double-breasted suit and accompanied Grandmother on a boat excursion. In the photographs he stands close to her as she looks over the rail, away from him. They are stylish, slender, and unsmiling. In another picture he carries a rolled newspaper in his hand. He looks to the side and stands awkwardly. He looks like a haunted man, despite his fine clothes.

In all the photographs Grandmother wears a hat, gloves, and heels. She sent luxury clothes back to Kansas for my older sister Mary to wear—mink collars, rhinestone pins, and cashmere sweaters. They were in my mother's closets for years after Sister left for California herself. Perfect style was my grandmother's specialty. These photographs also show a close woman friend, perhaps one of the cousins, with Grandmother, also dressed to the nines. These are stark photographs, with no community or family around except for this one friend. During their time in California my grandparents were at a distance from all their children and grandchildren. Yet they managed. They stayed until our grandmother reached mandatory retirement age.

Back in Kansas, they lived with my parents in Emporia, when I was a baby. Then they moved back to Newton, to a small downtown apartment near their son. Grandfather worked odd jobs in these latter years. They seldom spoke about their time in California. Photographs of another, more glamorous life are all that remain.

❖

19. Jane (Dotson) Ciabattari, the author's sister, and the author, ca. 1995, in Lawrence, Kansas. Author's collection.

City directories of the 1950s show some of my grandfather's last employment: taxi driver and liquor store clerk. My grandparents rented rooms above the taxi stand on the main street. They had no car, but they could walk to downtown stores, and when Grandfather worked for the taxi company, they had transportation. In his last job Grandfather had access to discounts at the liquor store, and perhaps he began drinking more. A head injury might worsen, with headaches. Alcohol can ameliorate pain, but this medicine takes a toll.

In later years Grandfather seldom visited our family, but I remember each meeting. He was quiet, sitting in a chair without comment or even, it seemed, a breath. That did not mean he had no effect on everyone. I felt his presence; I felt the attitude of my mother toward him; I felt my grandmother's continuous minor key sorrow. During these 1950s visits we played cards together. He passed on gambling skills, which have helped me in many ways through the years. He passed on his stories about the KKK and union struggles. Never was he drinking when we were together.

One cold night on those grasslands hills barely contained by a grid of streets, after I went to bed, he drank with my father. When I awoke in the morning, no one spoke. I felt some afterimage burned in the air, like the moment after a lightning strike. My mother was angry at both of them and gave me the impression both had imbibed.

That night ended in a contentious argument. My mother entered into the fray, and she was full of fury long afterward. Our grandparents never visited after that. In my bones I always knew the Greek arc of tragedy: events proceed to a final, unalterable destiny.

My dad once told me what a kind man Grandfather was, but drinking was his downfall. That was the theme of his later years. That is the last memory most relatives had of him, and in time it became the only memory, a broken stone man stretched out on a prairie hillside, fading with each winter's frost.

Only recently have I appreciated what an influence Grandfather

was on my father, who descended from British Isles and Cherokee abolitionists on one side and Confederates on the other. He
broke from his own father's Republican affiliation and become a
Democrat. He joined a union and became a leader, and he broke
with his father's more extreme Christian beliefs and acquaintance
with the KKK. Even though it was unspoken, Grandfather Bruner's
influence on the family continued through my father. I remember
my father telling me how every person, no matter what race, has
the same rights under the Constitution.

Father taught us to consider the welfare of the community and the
importance of service as an ideal, over individual profit, in contrast
to his businessman father's example. He became active in local politics, and his signature letters to the *Emporia Gazette* editor William
Lindsay White became famous as solo Democrat commentary in the
Republican town. In later years my father joined the county social
welfare board and the library board. He was a good son-in-law to
the maverick Native man, my grandfather.

They shared the vice of strong drink. I remember how my father
drank for days after their falling out. The two men had been friends,
and my father missed him.

A relative once told me, "I always knew Frank Bruner was Indian
because of the way he couldn't handle alcohol." Stereotypes are one
of the most insidious of Native difficulties.

I responded, "Why do Irish, French, Russians, and Germans
have such bad alcohol problems? Where is there a family without
such problems?"

In the middle years of the twentieth century a man's children
die, and he suffers chronic pain from a work accident. Effective
antidepressants and painkilling medicines do not exist. No twelve-
step programs exist. Civil rights laws are decades in the future, and
prejudice is a daily occurrence. My grandfather endured pain, and
he drank.

Grandfather, a lifelong smoker, developed lung cancer in 1962.
My mother worried as the disease wore him down. She and I and
my sister took the train to visit him several times in their apartment.

The grandparents' rented rooms in Newton seemed darker than ever those winter months.

The last time I saw him was soon after surgery. Grandfather took my mother aside and raised his shirt to show scars across his chest. Through the doorway I saw the jagged stitches on his skin. I realize now he tried to keep this disfigurement hidden from me, his granddaughter, by leaving the room. He did not want me to remember him as a wounded, dying man.

❖

I remember a visit to my grandparents' home when I was about ten, a few years before their deaths. This was a rare event. My mother left my brother, sister, and me with her parents for an hour or so. We were all awkward, as we hardly knew our grandparents by then. Grandmother served a meal of Campbell's Soup and sandwiches. My brother took charge and made a joke—"What? No chips in the china?" He made it clear this was nicer than home, and Grandmother smiled. We all laughed, relieved.

I recall how strained the atmosphere was, how my grandfather was in the other room with no explanation (the one time I suspect he was drunk), and how my grandmother's lips trembled. My brother, at sixteen, was the parent figure who eased the conversation along.

When I return in memory to that apartment, the rooms always seem unnaturally dark. I visited that downtown building recently, and it has an eastern exposure—so early-morning sun hits the window and recedes in a tidal wash of yellow light, leaving the rooms in a long twilight of sepia shadows. My memory was correct. On our afternoon visit we entered long shadows, when life seemed about to ebb away from our grandparents.

I appreciate their quiet heroism as they faced old age. At the end of their lives my grandparents struggled with decades of loss, yet they organized their lives to be independent. Basics of radio, newspapers, library books, and delivered groceries sustained them. My grandmother had regular rounds she made downtown to shop and perhaps to see friends at the lunch counters.

20. Evelyn (Miller) Bruner, Mary (Dotson) Marchetti, and Frank Bruner Junior in Newton, Kansas, apartment, 1960. Author's collection.

My California sister, Mary, visited them in 1961, about a year later, and she brought a television. This was a luxury item and surely a welcome gift for older people who seldom left home. Sister made the two-hour car trip with my brother to see them, and as much as I begged, I was not allowed to go. Brother took the last photograph of the grandparents, my sister, and the television. The Kodak flashbulb washes out half the picture, just like details of my grandparents' lives are partially lost in the family lore. My grandmother is almost invisible.

The photograph shows ornate wallpaper covering the walls, a sumac leaf pattern in sage green. No doubt Grandfather had wallpapered the simple apartment, as that was one of his skills. It created some beauty. Against that flat simulation of a forest, their lives continued.

Each day the sun still strikes the glass windows of their home, the apartment where once my grandparents rose, washed, dressed, and prepared for the day. Each day part of me is with them behind the glass as sun renews its light. I am an elder now, almost as old as my grandparents were in that apartment. I have traveled the four directions of life: birth, youth, middle age, and old age. Now I stand with my grandfather and grandmother in the fourth and last quarter.

Buildings have their own animus, and when they burn down, people mourn. The time my grandparents lived in that apartment, fifty years ago, makes the building a sacred site for me. The eastern windows are visible from the main street of Newton. I wish I could talk with my grandparents now and express appreciation for their gifts of life, courage, ethics, and hope.

❖

My grandfather walks toward me on the street in the 1950s. He dresses like anyone else on the Great Plains—trousers, plaid shirt, and sturdy leather shoes. His black hair is slicked back, trimmed a bit long and still full. His eyes look to the side as he minds his own business. Eye contact is much more purposeful in this region, and direct gaze is a conversation—either a greeting or a challenge. He moves unsurely on older bones and joints, but the sidewalk is familiar, and he has his routines.

His son visits weekly, but the grandchildren are busy elsewhere. His surviving daughter is immersed in her own family in another town. His wife and he are mostly alone, even though siblings live a few miles away. This is how I see Grandfather, in pain, and not just physical. His family is scattered. The Delaware lineage has broken apart.

As an adult, my mother became involved with her husband's wealthier, patriarchal family. She had a child, several difficult miscarriages, and then three more children. She did not visit her grandparents Charlotte and Frank Senior, who lived just a few miles away. After a move to Emporia, a short train ride east on the train, she seldom even saw her mother and father. Her past life, and all her Native relatives, receded as she assumed the role of a middle-class matron.

After fifty years I can speculate about the interplay of isolation, social displacement, and alcoholism in the life of my grandfather. He had been obstreperous as a boy, but then he had channeled energy into athletics. He had wandered among different jobs, but then he had settled into employment with the railroad until he was injured. He lost two children, a terrible blow, but he succeeded in raising the two who survived. His marriage continued, perhaps because his wife simply endured, but even after the years of disgrace, he and his wife enjoyed each other's company. I want to celebrate the successes he had and balance them with the difficulties. I want to see his face among the people I greet as I walk small town main streets in Kansas. My grandfather does not fit into the simple category of "drunk." Throughout my life I never saw Grandfather drunk, so he had the ability to remain sober. I felt the aftermath of one of his sprees, and I do not doubt alcohol was a problem. Probably his drinking was the reason why my mother avoided family visits, especially after the last family blowup. It was, however, a surface symptom of deeper issues.

Recent research details how head injuries make profound changes in people's behaviors. During Grandfather's lifetime this information was not available. Intermingling of genuine injury and alcohol abuse are impossible to tease apart so many years later, but the term *self-medication* adds another perspective. Stereotypes of Native people as alcoholics are still pervasive, so even Grandfather's own family members looked no further for explanation of his problems.

Historic trauma and *transgenerational trauma* are terms that describe continuing wounds of Native people's response to bias. This is another way to contextualize Grandfather's life. A check-list of historic trauma symptoms from the Aboriginal Healing

Foundation—"isolation and withdrawal; disruption in intimate relationships; repeated failures of self-protection"—outlines his biography.

My mother became isolated, like her parents before her. The habit of broken families continued, in a pattern of unconscious behaviors. This is a continuing internalized diaspora.

If I were to meet my grandfather as he passes me on the sidewalk of a prairie town, where the same buildings stand unchanged after generations, I would see a story of sorrow. It is evening. He ends his shift as a clerk in the liquor store and climbs stairs to a modest abode. Dinner awaits him, radio, and other small comforts, including whiskey. During these last days of his life Grandmother sent birthday cards in the mail, each with a dollar bill. Grandfather did not reach out.

❖

During the funeral of my Delaware Indian grandfather, I was shocked silent at the sight of the large wooden casket. I was thirteen and frightened of death. A handful of people sat scattered about the pews, but they gazed only at the priest as he chanted a psalm.

Lying at the front of the chapel, Grandfather was the center of attention yet also removed—present and absent at once, one of his usual tricks. The Episcopal priest ignored the dead man as he eulogized a lost penitent traveling to heaven, no one I recognized. The set order of the "Burial of the Dead" from the *Book of Common Prayer* was foreign to me.

I turned my attention to Grandfather's monumental oaken coffin. In the church he lay within the wooden centerpiece, with no flowers, so its grain shone uncovered. Auburn plumes swirled the length of it. I thought I saw a meandering flight of black birds tracing the smooth corners, lingering in the arabesques of frozen tree growth, but they disappeared. The rush of their wings was almost audible, like his words.

Grandfather spoke to me through my memories. He described downtown streets, his deceased baby daughters, cancer's unfolding, and the patience of wood as its patterns create double curves. I barely heard the priest complete the psalm: "For I am a stranger with thee, and a sojourner, as all my fathers were. O spare me a little, that I may recover my strength, before I go hence."

Responders' amens died away. The high register of the organ wheezed a recessional. All of us stood and waited for my grandmother to stagger down the center aisle with my uncle holding her arm. She was already halfway to the next world, and a few months later she would die and descend into the earth to lie by her husband's side.

In the church foyer I met one of his brothers—a dark, white-haired man, Uncle Harry, distracted, who barely nodded. My mother held my arm and whispered to keep quiet around this stranger. This is how I understood she was ashamed of her own family, including me, as she pushed me behind her. I should remain silent, muffle my conversation, and stay within my own invisible box, like my grandfather.

Later in the car my mother said, "Dad seldom spoke, but people listened when he did." She said nothing else, and I wondered if this was meant to be a compliment or not. Then she was unusually silent. On this one day she ceased her incessant talk. She did not think to explain death to my sister or me. This silence, at an important moment, was another aspect of her removal from emotional situations.

My sister Jane remembers this as her first funeral—"so painful," she wrote me in a letter recently, and "so much unspoken." She was sixteen. In my memory an odd amnesia occurs. I remember the casket, the uncle, Mother's tense silence—and not my sister's presence. The internalization of the isolation was so complete that I erased memory of my sister-ally. We did not discuss the experience with each other until recently.

Weeks after the funeral, I became afraid of dying in my sleep. If I did not pay attention, I also would become paralyzed, taken away from home, and put within a wooden container. Grandfather, one of the few adults who listened to me, was imprisoned underground as eternal punishment. I might be laid alongside him forever, and no one would notice our calls for help.

Now I understand how paralyzed he had been most of his life as he followed an unplotted course between a time when "Indian" wars were barely concluded and another time when Native people had recognized legal rights. His family missed the Delaware migration to Oklahoma by a generation, yet they identified as Native. They were like my grandchildren through marriage, who are not able to enroll as tribal members because of their mixed heritage. Their enrolled Menominee and Lakota parents raise them, so their ethnic identity is clear, yet politically they are not Native. This limbo is the fate of many Native people in the United States.

I hope Grandfather is not lost in a distant heaven beyond the sun but rather nearby, settled deeply in rich bottomlands mud of the Cottonwood River, in sight of each full moon and each day's sun. Turtles join him in the winter to share a living dormancy. In spring sun thaws the ice, and everything comes back to life. In this world his words continue to mingle with the morning mists. As they resound, they keep heaven and earth in motion.

PART 2

Cutting Ties

Dorothy Bruner Dotson (1915–2002)

Eva (later known as Evelyn) Bruner returned to her parents' house in Kansas City for delivery of her first baby. On October 27, 1915, the thirteen-pound daughter, Dorothy Lea Bruner, drew her first breath. The new baby was almost bald. Grandmother tied bows on her fuzz-covered pate to prettify the little girl. Finally, black wavy hair with chestnut highlights grew in, neither her mother's blonde curls nor her father's straight ebony hair, but instead a cross-blend. My mother resembled neither of her parents. All her life she went her own way.

At first many family members surrounded the little girl. Maternal grandparents Edmond and Catherine (Tomlinson) Miller lived a few blocks west of the Delaware and Wyandot neighborhoods. Edmond was both Irish and German, from Illinois by way of Ottawa, Kansas. Mary Catherine, or "Cap," was of Irish descent, from Vermillion County, Illinois. She earned the nickname Cap, short for Captain, because she ruled her household with military order. She also had prophetic dreams, another reason to obey her. When she dreamed her husband could be killed in a train wreck, the next day he quit his railroad job. Indeed, according to the family legend, his train

21. Frank Bruner Junior with his firstborn child, Dorothy Lea Bruner, 1915–16. Author's collection. Gift of Gail Bruner Murrow.

derailed. This intuitive sixth sense is another family inheritance. My mother always knew what I was hiding from her since she had extra awareness of all people around her. She craved time alone to separate her own feelings from those of others. Only when she was elderly did she attend church, at the early morning services, when her hypervigilance would be less taxing. I suspect this sensitive nature came from her Grandmother Miller.

Cap Miller was a lifelong Presbyterian. Not much else is known about her, not even her parents' names. Her youngest daughter, Frances, had a chronic lung condition, probably cystic fibrosis. Care of this invalid cast a pall over the Miller household. The birth of a healthy grandchild must have been a joyous distraction.

My mother told me how important a daughter's birth had been to her father's family, the Bruners. Mother had no Delaware girl cousins or even aunts. While other families celebrated the birth of sons, matrilocal Delaware people depended on the female line. Grandmother Charlotte was her closest Delaware female relative, and in the future, they spent a lot of time together. Birth of a girl was welcomed.

So, Dorothy began life as the center of attention within the extended family. Grandparents, uncles, cousins, and her parents doted on her. Her mother and father posed with the baby in individual portraits. In one photograph Frank seems especially delighted with his firstborn child, as he looks into her eyes.

The new daughter was willful, smart, energetic, and finicky. She must have been a fussy child. She had an acute sense of smell, so bad odors bothered her. Sounds also could bother her. She heard distant tones acutely, and blaring noises were painful. Her high-strung nature must have kept everyone on edge. She was an only child for eight years, and for the rest of her life she expected to be the focal point of any conversation. She had little curiosity about her support cast but, rather, saw herself as the star performer.

She had only superficial interest in her family and knew little about her origins. She knew nothing about the hybrid Kansas City community where she was born. This patchwork of communities resembled eastern Oklahoma, another former Indian Territory, as Delaware tribal member Lynette Perry describes: "Delaware, Cherokee, white, Osage, it didn't much matter to us. We pretty much accepted our neighbors as folks, even did a lot of intermarrying." I never heard any hint that Frank Bruner and Eva Miller's marriage in Kansas City caused any clash. In contrast, across the river in Kansas City, Missouri, the tradition of slavery lingered.

Miscegenation laws were in force until the 1960s. As a result, many mixed-race people chose to live in Kansas City, Kansas, where tribal communities persisted.

The Kansas River flows through my mother's birth town and joins with the Missouri River, so bottomlands animals populate the terrain. In early summer bullfrogs bellow from the shallows, and blue herons wade the creeks. Many varieties of turtles—snapping, softshell, painted, slider, mud—navigate the muddy banks, and some of them must have found their way into the Bruner cookpot. The legs, neck, and tail are rich stewing meat. Subsistence fishing and gardening can provide basics of a family's sustenance but no cash income.

Soon the new father looked for work. For years he had no permanent position. A city directory lists him as a stenographer before his marriage, so he had office skills, but he did not continue with office work. For a brief spell he owned a repair garage, but that failed. Perhaps alcohol was a factor in his instability, but my mother never indicated it was a problem when she was a child. She remembered her father as a practical-minded craftsman who took pride in a job well done. At this distance in time the simplest answer to his employment trouble is his ethnicity. My Native husband encounters prejudice regularly. In western Kansas, not far from Grandfather's home, he recently went into a truck stop to pay for gas and was treated badly—glares and snide comments. This was a not-so-subtle twenty-first-century lesson. If Grandfather did not act subserviently, he no doubt experienced consequences. Underemployment is a pernicious aspect of racism.

As they moved around, my grandmother set up housekeeping in one rooming house after another. After a few years, further difficulties occurred when her second pregnancy ended tragically with the death of one twin and with the second twin terminally ill. This was a hard time, as her husband sought work in California, Kansas City, the Great Plains, and back in Kansas City. They finally settled in Newton, Kansas, not far from Burns. Perhaps family connections or old neighbors helped him find employment. He became a brakeman working in the rail yards for the Santa Fe railroad, good pay for the region. His job was protected by unions.

In Newton, as Dorothy started school, she enjoyed the most prosperous part of her parents' lives. Railroading was a respected job, so the family had an above-average place in the stratified social scale of the small town. They could afford an arts and crafts style house in a middle-class neighborhood. As she grew up, my mother enjoyed a circle of close girlfriends. This was the best time of her life, she told me later, before adult responsibilities. She attended the Episcopalian church and loved the social activities. She told me several times that she liked Episcopalians because the Methodists could not dance. By the age of twelve she had met my father and flirted with him. I never saw my mother dance, but she commented on what a skilled dancer my father was during their teen years. His uncle owned a jazz club in Wichita, where they and their friends were welcome. This successful teenage interlude is what Mother remembered about her childhood, not the family difficulties after high school.

At home her mother cooked, sewed, and gardened. Her mother served rich meals, when a milk cow was part of the household economy. Hand-churned butter found its way into desserts, sauces, and table spreads. She relished food all her long life.

At sixteen Mother attended a summer camp, Mary-Dell Camp, in nearby Abilene, Kansas. From there she wrote home in July 1931, "I'm coming along keen in rifling." She passed the pro-marksman award and was about to start her next higher rating. No doubt her father had given her early shooting lessons. Perhaps Grandmother Charlotte shared her derringer. My mother excelled at croquet and rowing, but swimming was a challenge. She wanted the highest rating in every activity, at camp or on the lake. "I'm getting as brown as an Indian," she wrote, in an ironic reference to her dark complexion. She described the food, her friends, and sharing a cabin with seven girls. "I'm having the swellest time I've ever had," she concluded. Some of the camp counselors were young college women, and she clearly admired them. She could see that college

22. Dorothy (Bruner) Dotson, age sixteen. Photograph taken in Newton, Kansas, 1931. Author's collection.

was the next benchmark. She already loved school and competed for the highest grades.

She addressed her parents and little brother in this letter; sent greetings to an elderly great-aunt, Hanna Bair; and ended affectionately, "Lots of love, Dorothy." I never heard her say "I love you" or anything intimate during my life, but at that time this was a casual sign-off. In these letters she seems confident and happy.

My aunt sent these letters to me after Mother died, or I would never have known about this camp experience. A gap occurs between these letters and high school graduation. I remember only my mother's stories of poverty during the Depression, not the extravagance of a summer camp. Mother told me that her parents could not afford to send her to college, so she qualified for a scholarship. When the stipend ran out, as the Depression deepened, she had to quit college to work in a doctor's office. She prided herself on this work and studied Latin medical terms to improve her performance.

My father and mother paired off in high school, she told me, because they were the two smartest kids in the class. They dated others until they were juniors, when they became a serious couple. His parents were well-to-do and lived in a grand house in the best part of town. They approved of her, she told me, because she did not drink. In his teens my father already had trouble handling alcohol. She said, "I just liked Coca-Cola." She never tasted alcohol, but this early-twentieth-century concoction of sugar, caffeine, and spent coca leaves suited her. The company has since changed the formula.

When my unmarried parents were eighteen, my father's wealthy family took her with them to Colorado for a chaperoned vacation. Mother loved the mountains. It was a welcome excursion she could not otherwise afford. When she and my father turned twenty, in late 1935, they eloped. This spared her parents the expense of a wedding, she told me.

My mother never discussed her parents' ethnicity or Grandfather's deepening health issues, only that they were poor. One of my mother's strongest qualities was denial. She never said anything critical about her father, only brief praise. He was patient. He was skilled at woodworking. He never raised his voice. He never ever spanked her. Despite her faint praise of her own family, she looked forward to being part of her husband's established business family. They would move into his parents' home, not hers.

When I asked about her maternal grandparents in Kansas City, my mother described them in the vaguest terms. Grandfather Miller had beautiful penmanship and worked as an engraver in a department store. Grandmother Miller tended the ill daughter. My mother did not explain her later alienation from all her grandparents, what catastrophe triggered it or what gradually eroded those relationships. She lived a more and more isolated life, which began with her marriage and continued as her own relatives drifted into the background.

After marriage my parents lived only briefly in the fine house of the wealthy in-laws. One afternoon the young brother-in-law told my mother what a nuisance she was. My mother was furious, and she insisted that they move out the same day. She vowed she would never set foot in her mother-in-law's house again, and she did not. Again, one incident tipped the balance of pent-up resentments, and the family fractured. The in-laws, nonetheless, ruled their lives for several more years. They paid for a small house for the young family. Mother's father-in-law insisted she quit her job in the doctor's office. "He couldn't let people know his son was not capable of supporting a wife," she told me. She obeyed. Unfulfilled career plans became a major theme in her life, until she returned to college in her fifties.

During the first days of marriage my father worked in the family grocery supply business, which meant long days trucking fruit from Texas and Arkansas. His father treated him like hired help, not a junior partner. The pay was low, and any shortcoming brought sharp criticism. After ten years my father left the family business and took a job on the Santa Fe railroad. He followed the example of his father-in-law, Grandfather Bruner, rather than his own father. The Delaware man's influence had long-reaching effects, as my father learned to identify with workingmen, not management. Father would later turn down promotions to work as a manager.

A more complete break with the in-laws came when my parents moved to Emporia, eighty miles away. This small town on the eastern edge of the Flint Hills was very similar to Newton. The main attraction was an established state college where they could educate their children, my mother told me. She did not mention how the conflict with in-laws played a role in their decision to put distance between them and their hometown. I see, nonetheless, my mother's strong will at work in this important decision and that my father had acquiesced.

They had a child immediately after marriage, Mary, and then several failed pregnancies. Six years later a boy survived, David; a girl, Jane; and then another girl (me)—all within thirteen years. My mother became immersed in the daily business of keeping a large household running, and this occupied her adulthood for thirty years, from 1936 to 1967.

When I visited home in the late 1960s, I saw her renewal of personal goals. She completed a bachelor's degree and started a master's. She taught college as a teaching assistant and filled in part-time at the high school. In the summers she gardened, cooked, and met with friends. After she completed her advanced degree, in her sixties, she relaxed a bit. She had achieved an important goal, but no employment opportunity existed after she reached the mandatory retirement age, before passage of the Age Discrimination in Employment Act of 1967. Even without a job, she gloried in her achievement and displayed a copy of her thesis to anyone who stopped by the house.

Her marriage gradually became less conflicted as my father quit resisting her outside activities. They shared some political and library groups. I remember her presenting a testimonial about my father as he ended tenure as the county Democrat association chairman. She was descriptive and funny. When my father had a debilitating stroke, she nursed him until his death seven years later.

Mother had no sense of being Native or European descended or both, in part because many of her friends were from similarly suppressed backgrounds. Eastern Kansas is a geography of mixed populations. Four reservations remain in Kansas. In Emporia, Mother's Canadian friend Annette Vincent was peculiar because of her endearing British quirks. Mother's other close friend, Ada Gilbert, traveled regularly to Ponca City, Oklahoma, for tribal events and expressed allegiance to her Native culture. My mother considered herself in-between: a melting-pot American. Her father's and mother's struggles were not her concern. Daily events filled her conversation as she talked compulsively whenever she could find an audience.

However much she ignored her family past, she was a result of generations before her. I remember how, as she conversed, descriptive gestures accompanied her commentary, similar to those of many Native people I know. "Tie a Kiowa woman's hands behind her back, and she can't talk," my friend Jennie once said. My husband wrote an article about the hand signs the Menominee sawmill workers developed, so signing continues to be part of that Algonquian nation's rhetorical style. But as a girl, I remember being embarrassed when my mother pantomimed so much of her conversation, unlike the more reserved neighborhood mothers. These were not emphatic stabs in the air. She sat with legs even, so her thighs created a table, and then she drew air pictures. People of many ethnicities gesture as they speak, but Mother's signing was not for emphasis, nor did she use commonplace gestures like a "thumbs up." Her brother also had this speaking style, so it appears their father taught his children implicit lessons, including a manner of presenting a conversation. Mother talked, with her gestures, about aphids on the roses or summer rains or sewing projects. She did not consider a conversation complete without her improvised hand motions.

My mother saw her parents less and less frequently. She had my father's problems to face every day, and avoiding another set of family issues simplified her life. She hosted her husband's elderly grandmother a few times, and I remember meeting this sweet-faced, gentle woman who smelled of face powder. Annual visits from my father's parents were tense occasions. Otherwise, few outsiders visited. All four of Mother's grandparents, who had been so delighted to see a little girl born in 1915, were forgotten, even though they lived into their eighties. It was as if they had never existed. She wrapped the wedding quilt her Delaware grandmother Charlotte had made in sheets and put it in a closet out of sight.

❖

From the first my mother and I were no match. Ironically, she loved images of the Madonna, so knickknacks of Mary with baby Jesus jumbled among magazines on end tables in the living room. Never did I live up to her expectations. She wanted me to be blonde, curly-haired, and bubbly, like my father's British Isles, Cherokee, and German family, but in 1949 I was born with straight black hair and blue-brown eyes, like her Bruner relatives. After six weeks, perhaps in an effort to please her, my hair turned wavy and light brown or dark blonde—*dishwater blonde* was the family term. My eyes turned muddy brown. My straight-haired eldest sister told me about burning permanents all her childhood, as our mother tried to make her resemble Shirley Temple. With natural curls I was spared that fate, but my eyes were not the desired blue, and my hair was "brunette." Somehow I knew these features were less desirable.

Our mother often became enraged at me and my siblings. Early on I felt the whack of her yardstick like a puppy in a litter. Years later she would tell me how her own father had never laid a hand on her, how he would take her roller skates and put them up high as punishment, how he explained everything very patiently. She never seemed to notice the non sequitur, the contrast between her upbringing and the way she punished her own children. She raged, like winter storms blew through our wood frame house. Her frustrations were unconscious forces, turned into thunderbolts that could strike without warning. Details of her subliminal traumas are missing, but the results were dramatically visible.

For me her temper was a fundamental fact of life, incomprehensible until I learned undercurrents of the family history. She talked once about being called "Frenchie" at school because of her "olive complexion," as she described herself. This was all she would say.

I asked if she were Indian once, but her curly hair, she explained, made it clear that she was not. She thought her father might be, but her identity, in her mind, was a separate matter. Her parents were poor, and marrying well, in her mind, had changed her identity.

Unexpectedly, her husband's family fortunes changed for the worse. She found herself no better off than her mother, with tasks of cooking, dishwashing, and cleaning. She cranked endless piles of laundry in the manual washing machine. Money was tight, and there was no car. She was trapped.

Mother displayed double personalities. She was pleasant and chatty for the neighbor at the door. As soon as the door shut, though, she snarled at me. Even when she seemed calm, I knew it would not last. As a child, when she yelled or yanked my tangled hair into braids, I pulled within myself. I found succor in relationships with my three older siblings. We resisted our mother's rule in an unspoken conspiracy. The sibling relationships were paramount, as my mother taught us, but this had unexpected consequences for her as we banded together. She was outside our circle.

My older sister Mary cooked with me, sang, played games, and called me her "little monkey." Every Saturday she listened to opera on the radio and baked pies while I "helped." She was the mother-sister I adored. My brother taught me wrestling moves, knife throwing, cards, and rules for football. Sometimes he persuaded me to clean his room so our mother would not unleash her anger, and I did whatever he said, even performing hated chores. Once when Mother struck him with a hairbrush, I ran at her with my fists flailing. I could not stand to see my brother hurt. This one time she thought I was cute and laughed. I felt a child's sense of justice and great relief.

My other sister, Jane, just three years older, stayed with me morning to night, as we avoided our mother. We played dolls and house and jacks and jump rope. When we were old enough, we read novels and discussed adventures of *Little Women*. We talked about when we would be famous writers ourselves, like authors of our favorite books. We both have enjoyed writing as a vocation.

She was an invaluable companion, except during my long, solitary rambles outside.

Another comfort was my father's library: brightly colored children's books, *Reader's Digest* books, Asian philosophy (*Tibetan Book of the Dead* and yoga), fantasy (Conan, Tarzan), Mari Sandoz's biography of Crazy Horse, Nancy Drew mysteries, science fiction, history (C. W. Ceram, Will Durant), nature (Rachel Carson and Thor Heyerdahl), and every other genre. I discovered that sweet trance induced by good writing. These were my escape from household tensions, an obsession as compelling as any other addiction. Perhaps books saved me from having much interest in alcohol. Others went to high school "beer busts" in the country where kegs were available, but for me books were the best distraction.

One night I read Twain's *A Connecticut Yankee in King Arthur's Court* for hours before my mother caught me. However she upbraided me, she could not take away my profound pleasure in those blissful hours. Like Tarzan, who navigated a violent jungle and survived surly gorillas, I maneuvered the hazards of my household and vested my emotions in the playacting of fiction. Reading and then writing were assertions of my separate identity. Gregory Orr writes about the healing role of literature, its ability to keep overwhelming emotions at a safe distance: "Survival begins when we 'translate' our crisis into language—where we give it symbolic expression as an unfolding drama of self and the forces that assail it." Binge reading helped me buffer the tensions between me and my mother. My beloved siblings and a shelf of books helped me survive well enough. My mother was a necessary hazard, like a busy street or a snowstorm. She led a very consistent life, and I appreciate that security. Bedtime was always nine o'clock. She enforced that rule like all the others, firmly and without any show of affection.

Once we talked indirectly about her aloofness. She described it in terms of her own father, how he had not made a show of his feelings. It was not in his character to make superficial assurances, she explained. His actions demonstrated his love for his family.

She concluded by saying she had married a man like her father, who also did not make a great show of his feelings but, instead, demonstrated reliability. This was as close as she came to explaining her own undemonstrative nature.

In addition to other pressures, my mother must have had very mixed feelings about gender roles. Her family had taught her to be an active, assertive woman, in keeping with Native expectations. At school she received higher grades than most of the boys in her class. As she grew up, she saw them take leadership roles, while she had few choices of vocation, and it galled her. History was her passion, something her father discussed with her as easily as the weather. This was not considered ladylike in those days. After Mother finally returned to college, years before the term "nontraditional" student was being used, she majored in one of the accepted fields for women—home economics. Her master's thesis, though, was a history of costume design. It was as close as she could come to her preferred field of study.

During these post–World War II times Rosie the Riveter was no longer a woman's role model. Doris Day movies revised women's roles into homemakers. Gender roles were still somewhat fluid in rural areas outside of town. In the Flint Hills of Kansas farmwork demanded participation of all family members. Many women tended cattle and drove farming machinery. Some assisted with huge meals for harvesting crews. Most could ride horses and shoot stray rattlesnakes that might wander onto the porch. Stories of regional characters such as Annie Oakley and Calamity Jane were historic proof of women's abilities. Delaware tribal member Lynette Perry describes the gender roles of rural Native women when she remembers her mother, "Mama was the daughter of a time and place that held Annie Oakley to be a model woman, and she could shoot a gun and ride a horse with the best of them." In the country women worked alongside men, but in town occupations were more strictly divided into men's work and women's work, with exceptions. In Emporia women's rights quickly made inroads in the 1960s. A woman joined the men's garden club, and the men made room for her. An African American woman became an administrator at the local college.

My father gloomily predicted social disaster in the 1970s as women "abandoned their children" for jobs. He grumbled that other German fathers—he considered himself German only—were absolute dictators in their homes, so why wasn't he? He could not, in any way, stop my mother's stubborn oppositions. When he refused to invest in a stone patio, she did the heavy landscaping work herself. She twisted a red bandana around her forehead and went to the country to find stones. These she lifted into the car trunk, transported home, and stacked. Then she dug out the entire patio area, laid a bed of sand, and fitted the stones together. In her seventies she still painted the house and fence.

Her father had taught her carpentry, so Mother did house repairs. We moved to a new house when I was five, a California ranch house not quite large enough for a family of six, but it was owned, not rented. My mother decided to construct cedar shelves into her closet, so she wrote to her father for help. He traveled from Newton and stayed a week. He built my mother a miter box, which became one of her prized possessions. As they worked together, never did I consider it odd for a woman to be carrying lumber or pounding nails. My father stepped back and watched. He provided income with his job, and the house was her domain.

Unconsciously, I followed my mother's example and developed independence outside women's roles. When I could drive a car legally at age fourteen, I did errands and eventually had a job as a mail carrier one summer. I cruised country roads and learned to enjoy the open expanses.

Despite the tensions in our family, the countryside was amazing. The Flint Hills have never been plowed; they are 80 percent of the remaining tallgrass prairie in the world. In my early teens I often biked to the Neosho River dam, about two miles away, and spent happy hours sifting through crinoid fossils, broken arrowheads, and gravel. History worked its way to the surface of the ground every time it rained, so I became curious about geology.

The Flint Hills edged our town, where our house was. Throughout the seasons about two hundred different kinds of wildflowers
bloomed. Bird families teemed in our backyard. My knowledge of
natural interconnections comes from the flora and fauna that grew
around me in those years. I watched watercress grow in lime-green
pads around the front porch drainpipe, where sun never touched.
Sunsets smeared the sky with cerise or tangerine or orchid. Winter
skies were delicate lemons and grays. In this Willa Cather grassland
I learned awe. Navajo people have a saying, "The Earth is a mother,"
and like them, I believe this is a literal truth. I cannot imagine my
life without those years of healing interaction with wildflowers, sky,
and free space. I went outdoors every day, and that was the time
when I felt loved by something larger than any human mother.

What my mother did for me, despite our disconnection, was to
practice benign neglect. She allowed me to roam in this landscape
of lessons. Natural laws disciplined me in ways I could not accept
from her. On our starboard side of the Flint Hills, where gales
explode in epic proportions, relationships within the web of living
beings is most vivid.

Underneath all her frustrations my mother centered her identity
within nature. She told me I had growth "stages," similar to seasons.
These were part of the natural cycle, not personal failings or sins.
At the time I resented her monologues and angry outbursts, but
now I appreciate that she did not frame my childhood with harsh
judgments.

As I grew into my teens, Mother and I found a common ground—
her love of gardening. From spring to late fall she immersed herself
in grapevines, strawberries, asparagus, dogwood, iris, Memorial
Day daisies, roses, hollyhocks, lemon balm, sweet rocket, Shasta
daisies, and chrysanthemums. This was a place where control was
more possible than uncertain family relationships, for both of us.

She told me the plot outside my bedroom window was my own
garden, and there she planted hen and chickens. Small round shoots
grew from a center rosette, broke off, and became new plants. This
was her model of mother and child, more real than the pietà figures

on the living room mantel. She took me with her to visit other gardeners in the town. I loved the exotica—extravagant banks of daffodils in the spring, and then in midsummer came stretches of day lilies. She taught me by example to value beauty—the nuances of iris beard colorations or delicate striations of tulips. She talked about plants as though they were family members. This may not be ideal socialization, but it worked well enough. I learned not to step on plants and how to give a wide berth to rose brambles, who resembled the grouchy neighbor across the street.

My mother introduced me to a living historic tradition of gardening. I overheard women's discussions of soil, hybridization, and weather. Some neighbor women were quite elderly, from the covered wagon days, so I also learned local history, another dimension of the land. Many had Native heritage. My mother's friend Ada talked about how "her people" gardened, sharing techniques of the tribal peoples nearby. The two traditions blended in the common ground of gardens. Everyone kept vegetable gardens as a matter of course.

When my children were born, they were the first of my mother's grandchildren to grow up near her, and she cautiously offered help. When she held my son for the first time, she tried to explain how she felt such satisfaction, her youngest child now mother of a baby. Despite our differences, she demonstrated for me a biological connection among the generations that transcends greeting card slogans.

During these years I gained insights into my mother's own mothering values. When my first son played with blocks for an entire afternoon, she praised him for having a "good attention span." I had not thought of that quality as anything worth nurturing, but I remembered how she had allowed me to stay with my toys uninterrupted. In this way she developed my inner sense of direction, a quality that allowed me to withstand the difficulties of my growing-up years.

My mother used a vocabulary with my babies I had never heard before, as she called my baby "cunning," in an Elizabethan usage, probably from her mother. She played baby games. She taught me how to pace the babies' days and to provide for their exercise.

She encouraged me to value their independence as they matured. Implicitly, she approved developmental stages for her adult daughter as well and for herself as an elderly woman. She encouraged memories of my own childhood as my babies matured. I teased out intercultural aspects of her identity through the years and learned to value what she passed forward to her children and grandchildren.

❖

Once, when I was four, my mother made matching dresses for my sisters and me, embellished with gold zigzag rickrack appliqué. I loved the full skirt and danced around and around in it. I twirled to see the horizontal circle of cloth ripple in waves. In the unconsciously racist term of the day, these were "squaw" dresses, an Algonquin term. It and the word *rickrack* were wonderful rhymes in my mouth. My delight made my mother happy.

Recently, a Menominee spiritual leader sewed a full, tiered skirt for me, similar to the one my mother had made. Her prayers went into every stitch, and each time I wear it, I feel her blessings. The skirt's circle is a universal symbol of wholeness, with a woman at the center. As a child, I wore skirts for "dress-up." My mother often wore a man's work clothes in the garden or for household chores, but for public occasions she wore women's apparel, and she expected the same for me. Dresses taught me my identity as a small woman and the potential that I might one day create life myself. On ordinary days I was free to wear jeans, but church required dresses.

Both of my parents fit Christianity to their needs in a much more relaxed way than fundamentalist neighbors. This reflected the mix of traditions in our household. We shared the potluck meals at the nearby Congregational church, and I remember our Bruner grandparents accompanying us to these "covered dish suppers" on rare occasions. My mother remained Episcopalian, so she seldom went to any services until her children were grown. Some of her family never belonged to a church. My father required that we children attend church, often alone. We were taught to pray daily to ourselves as private responsibilities.

We observed the holidays in dresses. Easter, Thanksgiving, Christmas, and New Year's Day all meant family feasts with proscribed dishes. Grace before these ritual feasts were our only family prayers. We celebrated spring, summer's harvest, dark winter solstice, and the sun's turning back to us in the seasonal sequence.

Girls' dresses were gender markers, as were dolls and playing house. Neighborhood boys in trousers joined us in this make-believe family play. Also, some boys' activities were part of girls' childhoods. Whittling was taken for granted as a daily skill. When I was five, my brother's pocketknife was an object of my envy. He sharpened sticks and flung it about the yard. In time I got my own, a small folding knife with a brown handle. The knife was an important implement that signified my maturity. I took it fishing and practiced whittling techniques. My whittling was as unskilled as my sewing, but it gave me confidence. I felt more prepared for adulthood.

Always, our mother sent us outdoors for long hours, despite the harsh weather. In the heat of summer we used the hose to create small pools and wallowed in the muddy dampness. After rain fat worms lay exposed on sidewalks, wriggling in our fingers when we plucked them from concrete cracks. Cicadas buzzed around us — small monsters erupting with noise. After frost bright scarlet and lemon leaves created a new playground, where we raked crunchy piles into forts. This natural realm was the most important textbook of my childhood.

I grew up in the midst of huge technological changes. Sputnik was launched in 1957, when I was eight, and then came the first United States astronauts. At the time we realized these harbingers of the future were momentous but distant. Our daily lives repeated, in most ways, cycles of the past. My mother dressed me in snow pants for sledding in zero-degree weather. She spent hours making dress-up outfits for my sisters and me. We were most like her beloved dolls when we held still and let her fit us with fabric. At those times we had her undivided attention.

❖

My mother might have loved dolls more than us children. She spent hours sewing for them, and their embroidered clothes were more ornate than what we wore. She sent to Kansas City for the best brand of dolls, Madame Alexander, with no expense spared. At Christmastime she became irritable from sewing late into the night, as she made tiny skirts and matching jackets for Betsy Walking Doll or the pixie Wendy. When we opened packages, I learned to feign appreciation for yet another doll's outfit.

When she was in her seventies, I asked my mother about her dolls and why they were so important. Even then, she displayed favorites on prominent shelves.

"When I was a little girl, Grandmother Charlotte said I could have as many dolls as I wanted," she said. "She took me shopping in downtown Kansas City in the fancy department stores, and she never complained about cost." I imagined these expeditions on streetcars across the river to towering buildings, not unlike my own early trips to Kansas City in the 1950s. I wondered how her grandmother limited her from buying out the store.

"She taught me how to hold them carefully and dress them," she continued, "and never let their clothes get dirty. We made sure my dollies had new clothes every year." She sighed. "She was the best grandmother. I just loved dolls ever since." This early experience of my mother shows how some moments in a child's life are preserved amid the commonplace stream of activities. The dolls triggered that one memory for my mother, with associations of her Delaware grandmother's excitement.

Some Native groups associate dolls with witchcraft, but for Delawares, dolls connote spiritual balance. Traditionally, certain women kept a male and a female doll wrapped carefully in a bundle. At harvest they unwrapped them for a holiday feast. Doll keepers cleaned the tiny figures, shined their silver brooches, and repaired worn cloth. Dolls were fed ceremonial meals as part of this annual celebration. Lynette Perry describes how her grandmother was among the last Delaware doll keepers in her memoir: "The legacy of many centuries is not so easily disposed of. Cultures are more resilient, tradition has a stronger hold on us, for all the styles that changed. The buried dolls come back, in different forms, to lend their healing power." This persistence of culture took form in my mother's love of dolls.

Grandmother Charlotte was not a traditional Delaware doll keeper, as far as I know, but she continued the custom of renewing her dolls. My mother learned this tradition, even if she no longer understood the cultural past. Her force of character no doubt imbued her miniature people with her imprint. She insisted on having several boy dolls as partners to the girls, unusual in those days, and I wondered why. I did not play with them, yet they had a power. As Perry explains about dolls she made, "I . . . felt their power without quite understanding it." The Delaware tradition included male counterparts.

My mother remembered her grandmother's doll legacy with her own observance. After a busy summer my mother healed herself each autumn by creating doll clothes. I think of her alone after her children were in bed, sewing tiny blouses by lamplight. Only now do I understand how this solitary labor sustained her. That was her true gift to our family at Christmas—she had made it through another difficult year.

My mother taught me how to make hollyhock dolls in the summer and corn husk dolls in late summer. She showed me how to sew simple blouse patterns for my larger doll. She saw to it that our grandfather built a dollhouse with elaborate furnishings for us girls.

When the weather turned cold, Jane, my sister nearest in age, and I spent long afternoons making our dolls act in long dramas. They would move from the dollhouse parlor to the kitchen and then upstairs to bedrooms, where they had nighttime dreams. I had many dreams that our dolls were alive and they were my friends.

After we grew up, my mother made Christmas doll figures for the grandchildren. She made sets of felt ornaments that were fairy-tale characters or birds of paradise or Christmas bears, usually in mated pairs. She sewed sets of redbirds, doves, favorite dogs, and angels. Each winter solstice we still unwrap them and set them around the

23. Dorothy (Bruner) Dotson, age fifty, in Emporia, Kansas, 1965. Photographed by H. C. Dixon at Granada Studio for the fiftieth wedding anniversary of Carrie (Strittmater) and William H. Dotson, Dorothy's husband's parents. Author's collection.

house. We eat sweets, salt, water, and meat, the four traditional elements of a meal. We eat oysters at Christmas, no matter how far we live from the ocean, and corn pudding. When I slice turkey for Christmas Eve, I use my mother's sharp steel-edged carving knife. My hands resemble hers more each year, with veins more prominent. At winter holiday meals, with her dolls around us, we remember my mother's indomitable life force. Our doll-keeping mother still exists, still potent.

As I write these memories, in the wickerwork of alphabetic reality, I conjure Grandmother Charlotte, my mother, and great-grandparents I never met. I am still playing dolls with my sister as I rebuild the dollhouse of our family. The dolls also are my children and grandchildren, existing in that floating interdimensional space of words, where they come to life when bidden.

❖

Into her eighties my mother kept a small garden of tomatoes, asparagus, squash, and green beans. The common pole beans can be eaten green or left to ripen and dry in the rows. These were the beans that Delawares and other Algonquian peoples use for winter storage. My mother also had a cutting garden of chives, spearmint, lemon balm, sage, thyme, and oregano. Often she planted the annual herbs—parsley, basil, and cilantro.

I was not surprised when, years later, my uncle told me about the large gardens my Delaware grandfather and grandmother tended. "Victory garden" was one term he used, from World War II, but even before that crisis, the habit of farming was ingrained.

My mother had her own memories of her grandparents' garden. She remembered sweet shelled peas from early vines that went so well with new potatoes and fresh cream. She imitated her family's example, and so do I.

When I was a newly married woman, I lived in an apartment with an attached garden, and there I planted the "three sisters"—corn, beans, and squash. I mail-ordered "Indian corn" because I wanted to see ears of red, blue, white, and yellow kernels. The

seeds arrived, I planted them, and they grew quickly. One night I
dreamed of them as people coming to life, one for each color. The
next morning I saw they had grown taller than the neighbors' sweet
corn. They had more scanty foliage and smaller ears, but the stalks
towered—perfect anchors for green bean vines. The variegated
kernels were shiny and robust. My neighbors considered them a
curiosity, along with my irregular rows interrupted by hills of corn.
These contrasted with their tidy plots measured out with string. But
I sensed the "ornamental" (so-called by the seed catalog) Indian
corn had strong vital force. I plant corn whenever I can, just as I
saw my mother do, and Indigenous varieties when possible.

Corn is natural in this part of the country, easily cultivated
along sandy river bottoms. Traditions remain from the old days.
My mother taught me to plant fish in each corn hill, small perch I
caught at a nearby pond.

In the Great Plains sunflowers are another staple, an important
source of oil. Some varieties have edible roots, "sun-chokes." An
Arikara woman told me how women planted several varieties of
sunflowers with corn along the river bottoms, then left for the
hunting season. When they returned in late summer, crops were
ready to harvest.

I always feel secure in my home area because of all the foods that
grow naturally or with a little help: amaranth, goosefoot (lamb's
quarters), pigweed, May grass, milkweed, and cattail tubers.

An area seed keeper, with an Oglala-Apache and Blackfoot and
Cherokee and Anglo heritage, is Dianna Henry from Jewell County,
Kansas. In her house are gallon jars filled with seeds: Cherokee flour
corn (*su-lu*), with large, white kernels; red popcorn; maroon Arikara
flint corn suited to the sandbars of shallow midwestern rivers; Osage
flour corn, which makes a purple flour; and dozens of others. Some
are ceremonial and not intended for people's food. In the freezer
she has more rare varieties, including Delaware blue flour corn,
adapted to the Northeast climate, with its short growing season.

Dianna Henry was the first person who helped me understand the
sophistication of corn development in the Americas. I recognized

then how my mother had such vast knowledge of gardening. She knew how to hybridize iris varieties. When my older sister was a teenager, Mother supported Sister's science fair experiments with hybrid strains. I went with them on some of the trips to trade iris with other gardeners. The old women were seed savers and wise in many ways.

Mother knew hundreds of plants, natural and domesticated, and how to care for each. Through the years she learned which varieties fared best in the extreme Flint Hills weather, with its high winds and limited rainfall. She grew corn every year because fresh corn was the best.

Corn was ubiquitous in my mother's kitchen, and she taught us to savor the fresh, green-tinted new corn, boiled quickly and eaten immediately. This was the best of summertime. Her holiday dishes included hot casseroles of corn enriched with cream or scalloped with beaten eggs. She also made corn pudding—a baked porridge of thick, salted cornmeal sweetened with molasses and currants. She bought cornmeal at the store and always had some on hand. It was essential in a kitchen, along with cornstarch as a thickener. We often had corn bread and sometimes a baked meat pie with corn batter baked on the top, which she called "tamale pie."

My mother served corn in some form almost every day. She kept alive recipes that were documented as early as 1654, when chronicler Edward Johnson described tamales: "Delicious cakes were baked by wrapping the moistened meal in husks of corn, and baking them under the embers." This was in Massachusetts, not the Southwest. Johnson went on to describe a basic corn gruel, still a staple known as "grits," but he called it "samp." He described stews made of parched corn, and the idea of cooking meat and grain together seemed novel to him. In 1683 William Penn described hominy, journey cakes (johnnycakes), and stews.

Food is the basis of ultimate social power. My Menominee husband uses food to explain the importance of women in his Algonquin-speaking nation. The clan mother decides how food will be apportioned. During famines she decides who will eat and who will die. No one can override her decision.

My mother and her friends exchanged starts of plants with each other and shared surplus vegetables. As a girl, I learned from my mother the empowerment of physical self-sufficiency. Food could be bought at the market, and also I could raise what I needed myself.

What we eat and digest enters into our bodies in very literal ways. Our stomachs are great cookpots that break down roughage and chemicals. Our bloodstreams dissolve this concoction and redistribute nutrients as fuel for growing flesh and bone. We are constructed of plants and animals, and often they enter our dreams. I remember the dream of the Indian corn I grew forty years ago, and still it is a powerful lesson from my mother and grandmothers and many great-grandmothers.

❖

My grandfather left a turquoise ring to my mother, one that he wore most of his life. He may have received it as a gift, but no story remains. The ring appeared in my mother's handkerchief drawer after her death, along with other valuables. She had never shown it to anyone. In the dark recess of the drawer, it was out of her sight, like her father's family. Yet it cast its spell.

When I visited my brother a few years ago, casually he mentioned the old turquoise ring Grandfather wore, how odd it was in our small Kansas town. "I always assumed Grandfather wore it because he was Indian," he said. Brother is older than I am and remembers more about Grandfather. "I never saw him when he wasn't wearing it," he said. "Whatever happened to it?"

I told him it was not lost. Even before I realized it was Grandfather's, I valued the ring as an heirloom and gave it to one of the grandsons. So, the ring continues its existence, still joined to the family.

Turquoise was my mother's favorite color to wear, and her dark hair and complexion showed well with its hue. As a child, she must have seen her father's ring daily, and perhaps that was a small but steady influence on her taste. She often wore a fancy turquoise dress she made for herself. When I saw someone at a distance wearing that bright color, I knew it would be her.

One of my mother's favorite garments was a Guatemalan jacket with turquoise, red, and yellow animals woven into its black background. It always hung on a nearby chair, ready to go with her out the door. The turquoise animals in the design faded to a lovely aqua color through the years. I came to associate that color and those animals with her; the coat was almost another layer of her skin.

In the grasslands we were surrounded by sky blue colors but no blues mixed with water—no teal or aqua or turquoise. Women wore pink or beige suits. Black was for mourning, white for brides. Turquoise was not in the McCall's pattern books and seldom in the fabric stores. Never was turquoise in Poole's Department Store dresses for grown women.

My childhood was an era when, instead of gemstones, women wore rhinestones. Or they displayed new plastic creations, such as Bakelite, a synthetic resin harder than amber. Bakelite bangles create a muted clack, part of the fashion statement. No one wore turquoise rings when I was a child, and men seldom did.

Once, when I was eighteen, I noticed a man wearing a turquoise ring, the Delaware man Don Ashapanek. I was working as a waitress in a soda fountain. When I served him, I noticed his turquoise ring was as large as my grandfather's. I overcame shyness to ask about it. He told me it was a gift from his aunt. He was a doctoral student at Emporia State University. Years later he was my colleague at Haskell Indian Nations University, and he still wore that family turquoise ring.

In the code of our small town, turquoise jewelry was "Indian," from faraway southwestern deserts. On occasion a wealthy neighbor would travel on the Santa Fe train and return with silver bracelets set with colorized aqua stones as souvenirs. No one seemed to ever wear them. My other grandmother brought me silver bracelets, embellished with turquoise, that fit my small wrists. They were delicate and feminine. The color popped brightly within the gleaming metal. I loved them, tried them on, and wore the dainty wristlets in the house. Turquoise, for me, is the color of gifts.

From recent books I learn the locations of turquoise mines in the Southwest. Each has its own colors, and some have lacy markings. My brother gave me a gift of a Lander Blue stone with a blue against black netting matrix. Leslie Marmon Silko writes about her personal attraction to the stone. All of its varieties obsess her, those that have been purchased as well as those she finds. Silko lives in the Tucson desert, where she walks daily and picks up nuggets from washouts. To her each is individual, with its own silent voice. I love her story about losing a favorite four-sided stone: "Even after I found three pieces of turquoise larger and as nicely polished as the small rectangular piece, still I searched the house for the lost piece. What is it about us human beings that we can't let go of lost things?" For Silko that stone has a quality not measured by size or polish. That stone has become necessary to her, and she cannot let it go.

My "lost thing" is my grandfather, and so I look for him in my mother's drawers and in turquoise jewelry. I find pieces, like Silko finds fragments of a larger turquoise rock ledge, and each is part of a larger epic. I imagine a time when my grandfather's life story was an intact seam of smooth, bright blues, like Silko's turquoise ledge that crops to the surface at intervals. This lode connects underground to a solid, unbroken river.

❖

After Mother's Episcopalian funeral my husband conducted a Native American Church memorial for her in our backyard. He arranged the family around a fire ring in generational order. Friends circled family and tended the fire. In turn we each spoke about her life. Then my husband burned her master's degree hood, which she had left folded in a closet, and her college diploma. The smoke rose straight into the winter clouds, toward the heavens of both traditions.

Mother and I were not at peace with each other in this world, but now, when I look over the funeral pictures—church flowers;

the cedar altar, eagle feathers, and Bible; the firewood brought by a friend; the circle of friends and family—I feel affection. She passed down wooden spoons, kettles, and white chinaware, part of my daily kitchen rituals. Her iris and day lilies bloom in my garden. One of the greatest surprises for me is how our relationship continues to evolve after her death.

As the charred ring of the memorial fire pit fades into new grass, I recover from shock. With her last breath she exhaled bright red blood, a vivid sight. For months I relived that moment. I felt the helplessness of not saving her. Now that image loosens its hold.

Recently I felt her ghost, or some similar presence, protect me. I was chopping onions with a cleaver, and it slipped. In an eerie moment I felt another person take the blade and put it in my other hand. I heard her voice, "Don't hurt yourself," as I must have heard it a thousand times when I was a baby.

I learned to get along without much emotional support from my mother years ago, so I do not miss the relationship as much as some daughters might. As the first years of mourning end, the guilt ebbs. One exact moment it was completely gone. It was in the garden as I tended violets transplanted from her garden. As I wrenched crabgrass from between their rhizomes, I saw my hand become her hand. Then I began to have memories of her laughter, and then bits of family stories returned. Now a word like *willow* reminds me of her war against the weeping willow tree that tangled our sewer line. *Hybridize* evokes her years patiently tending new strains of iris. It suggests her interest in joining various lineages in her four children.

Since her death I have found cousins and traded family stories that are eerily similar tales. We speculate about how claustrophobic small-town life puts pressure on people. Our parents worried about keeping up appearances so much that it stifled everyone. Official narratives of our families are like the crisp white sheets our mothers ironed weekly, without design or color. We cousins discuss how part of the midwestern ethos is based on fitting into community, at no small cost to individuals. We discuss the American Indian heritage in our family, how it was suppressed, and what that denial costs us to this day.

Different European identities also were uncovered. I learned how "German" Grandfather Miller was actually Irish, from a farm family. That rural Irish background was not acceptable to my mother either. She spent her life trying to fit into some ideal.

As pieces of my mother's life become clearer, I accept her more, along with her anxieties. Even after her death, my mother inhabits my memory, where I revise our relationship. Each time I recall her, different details seem significant. Perhaps this account can reclaim the story of her parents, especially the life of her Delaware father. I celebrate her survival through difficult years. I have learned patience with her, as I hope my children will have patience with my failings.

I find solace in the countryside that claimed her ashes. Another comfort is the sun, the same one my grandfather faced every morning in his apartment. The grasslands world is intense, and human differences become small in this space. In our small funeral fire pit we symbolically released Mother to the winds and the earth. Over two seasons the burned scar remains, smaller each year as green growth reclaims it. From my house the Kansas River is within view, about a mile away. It flows east through 1800s Delaware lands to Kansas City, where my mother was born. A band of green-leaved trees outlines the river until winter, when turtles hibernate and reeds dissolve in soil.

PART 3

A Haunted Life

Denise Dotson (b. 1949)

In each room of our three-story house, I found a safe place. From that spot, usually on the floor, I listened. When I was a small child, the Bruner grandparents lived in the third-story apartment of our seemingly infinite house. That distance seemed very far away. On special occasions they came into our kitchen for meals. Then my grandfather sat quietly in a side chair, slowly chewing his meal with false teeth. He drank coffee and dipped bread in it, to soften the hard crusts. He had his honored place, but he seldom spoke. I could see something was wrong but not exactly what.

On one occasion Grandfather and I were the topic of conversation, our resemblance to each other. We shared eyes that were as brown as the garden soil. He looked pleased, but we were both startled to be out of our usual roles. Words came at me quickly, too fast for response. We were grandfather and grandchild, minor players in our mixed-up, despairing, and occasionally joyful family.

Grandfather and Grandmother had returned from California about the time of my birth. They avoided their hometown, just eighty miles away. There they would face public disgrace for Grandfather's gambling indiscretions. At that time gambling was against the law in Kansas, and to many people it was sinful. Even worse, they were poor. Although I was a small child, I understood their postures of despair. My mother's burden of unfilled aspirations made her cranky, and daily contact with her poor parents made her situation more pronounced. My father staggered under financial responsibility for four children and now, to some extent, his in-laws.

My next older sibling, Jane, was three years older, very verbal, very pretty, and bright beyond her years. Today she is a brilliant writer. As a child, she was amazing. She entertained and distracted the family, full speed every day. With a quieter disposition I was a side attraction.

I worried over all the words I did not understand as well as the grown-ups' exclusionary experiences beyond the walls of the house. I seldom even went outdoors, and then only within our yard, so their descriptions were exotic, spoken in a foreign language of polysyllabic garble.

Because of his railroad job, my father was absent most days. When he was home, he bellowed rants about the outrageous pro-business positions of the newspaper editor William Lindsay White, the privileged son of William Allen White, a nationally known journalist. As the town celebrity, White spent much of the year in New York, where he published novels, memoirs (*Journey for Margaret*), and articles for the *New Yorker*. My father loathed his elitism. After long hours of labor and poor sleep, Father was surly, but that did not give my mother pause as she countered his diatribes.

I listened to everything: violent fights, orders for the milkman, rare and wonderful laughter, fabric store lists, warnings about weather—the 1951 Kansas City flood stands out, along with thunderstorms and blizzards.

I learned each conversation created different facial expressions, pacing, timbres of voice, lengthening of vowels for emphasis. The slow Midwest dialect uses tonal cues to add nuances, so a simple phrase such as "I'm late" can be a complaint, an apology, an accusation, or a question. The slow pace of this dialect allows for a great range of emotion. I learned to hear all the overtones and undertones of vocalizations, but I did not learn how to talk easily. I made mistakes, and everyone corrected me in a chorus, which made me even more withdrawn. Then my mother labeled me "tongue-tied," and the cure for that, she said, was cutting the tongue loose with a knife. I kept out of her reach as best as I could.

So in the early 1950s my grandfather and I sat silently as others around us chattered. He was sixty years old when I was born. As a boy, he had lived on the Cottonwood River in Burns, the same prairie stream that ran through our town to join the Neosho River. In the sweep of geography and time it was not distant at all. His history overlapped mine, in the grassy center of the continent. And so, through him, I have direct ties to the Indian Wars.

He was born just thirty-one years after a skirmish between Cheyennes and Kansas Indians in Council Grove, forty miles up the Neosho River. He was born twenty years after the Ponca man Standing Bear went to court in Omaha to assert his legal rights as a "person," not wildlife. The Poncas' route ran through Grandfather's hometown on their forced march to Oklahoma and again on the 1879 flight away from the horrors of that impoundment. These events were just a few paces ahead of us on trails that were still visible. Wagon ruts of the Santa Fe Trail passed near our town. Wounded Knee, the last of the Plains Indian Wars events, was a year after Grandfather's birth. He grew up in the penumbra of that violence against Native people.

Those events never entered our family conversation, but they existed as a presence in the air we breathed in that kitchen. In the early 1950s I grew up among people of the nineteenth century, the western frontier days, and they shaped my reality. I met some of the last Indian fighters, who described a gritty time of hardships, mean drifters, and short life spans. Neighbors and relatives had lived through rustlers, brawlers, and horse thieves. I remember my oldest sister, Mary, coming home from a ride on the city bus, during which she had sat next to an old woman who had grown up in a sod house, like our great-grandparents. These experiences seemed just a few days old.

When my grandfather did speak, everyone quieted down so his voice could be heard. The family showed its respect for him this way, and I watched this etiquette. Later I would learn that my father had more respect for him than his own father and how this affected all of us. One of the worst childhood sins was to interrupt. "Don't be impudent!" my mother would command, along with "Don't interrupt me while I'm talking!" We learned to never say "Shut up!" It was a breach of social rules to deny someone the right to speak and be heard.

I have lived in many different houses since that first home, and Grandfather moved out of the three-story house early in my life, but the family never left that first kitchen table. Grandfather's voice reverberates through time, even though his voice was soft. Even after I learned to talk, I kept his habit of silence.

❖

My memories commingle with early images of the church across the street. It was a trim, pink-brick Congregational church with a steeple tower piercing the brilliant blue heavens. This pointy European architecture was alien to the landscape, a contrast even to rambling gingerbread houses nestled into sloping streets around it. The cotton candy pink of the bricks was odd. As a child, I considered its existence as evidence of foreign countries, like palm tree villages shown in Sunday school pictures.

Despite its strange shape, the inside of the church was a homey place where we met friendly people. The minister of this independent congregation was a secular saint. When I was older, he would offer sympathy when family tensions erupted into battles. He never scolded the congregation about sinful ways, although once he noted more people worshipped at the nearby lake during summer Sundays than in the church. He was bemused, not angry. The two forms of celebration did not cancel each other out.

My grandfather and my grandmother lived apart from the minister's domain. They existed independently, suspended in our house's top floor, beyond high ceilings and endless windows. Years later my next older sister wondered at their seeming "exile" in the house. Most often we never saw them. Their third-story apartment was, I thought, our steeple. There above the trees time moved at a different speed. They had become old in distant attics in the eternity before I was born. I understood them as supernatural, like people in the Bible.

In that house near the church, I slept where branches of elm trees swayed just outside the window. This was an intact canopy, before blight killed the elms. Those attic rooms continue to exist as backdrop for my dreams. They are infinite nesting boxes, where I wander for hours and never tire. Sometimes my parents, brother, or sisters are with me. The painted lumber is birch bark white and still smells of sunshine. Odd buildings jumble outside the windows, but inside we are all together. We are safe. Some nights my grandparents reappear like moonlight flowing through the window panes, and time ceases to exist.

One night when I was not yet two years old, I had a flying dream, where I easily moved about the different floors of the house, soaring up and down the staircases. The next morning I ran to the head of the staircase leading the kitchen. I could smell buttered toast. I stood there transfixed, hungry, about to jump for a long moment. Something seemed different, though, something I could not name but something very real. Finally, I called for help to be carried down the stairs. I had come so close to leaping off. Instead, after long thought, I decided to believe in gravity.

Another time I remember my grandfather's profile reflecting in a window, a double image. He was looking at me closely because I am the only grandchild with his cleft chin. My mother said, "See how she inherited your mark." His smile was twisted, composed partly of pain, which I sense but cannot identify as easily as gravity.

Another memory from those days was when he taught me to drive, another kind of flight. I am a toddler, and he props me behind the wheel. At first I am terrified—I could hurt someone with this contraption. I squirm, but he encourages me. Then I put my hands on the wheel, turn it, and feel a surge of power. My powerful grandfather wants me to steer. I still have dreams about taking charge and driving buses. I never have dreams of being driven.

Steeples, stairs, windows, cars—all of them were spatial objects that defined the limits of my physical reality. Grandfather, the minister, my parents and siblings—all of these beings are aspects of my birth home, an infinite human construction that I revise with each memory.

❖

Houses are our turtle shells, and within them we are alive in a suspended, sheltered time. From Grandfather I learned to look for meaning in corners of conversations. Because we watched, we knew how nervous hands can tell more stories than words. I learned how families gather within house walls to converse in private, sometimes wordless ways not possible in pink-brick churches. From his patience I learned how to trudge forward and, no matter what, keep going.

Perhaps Grandfather spoke seldom because his ears were attuned to another language, one that hardly existed in its full form. He had the rhythm, the social forms, the gestures, but not the vocabulary or grammar of Delaware.

As the youngest child, I never could speak as well as anyone else, but as soon as I could, I wrote, and the page became my audience, a silent partner that always listened. In time I wrote letters to all my grandparents. Grandfather Bruner never wrote back, but that did not matter to me. I knew he was there, opening my envelopes. My mother continued to insist that I write him, so I did. Perhaps this writing about him is a continuation of those letters I once sent to his address, general delivery in Newton.

In fourth grade a teacher showed us how to write poetry. I composed a verse about the redbird in the backyard, the one I exchanged whistles with, mimicking its piccolo language. Then I started keeping a diary and next a journal. All these I kept hidden from my family, my own form of double silence. As my mother raged or gave approval randomly, I had control over what I wrote.

Indeed, I spoke so seldom that I did not have an accent like anyone around me. When I had my first job at a local soda fountain, people thought I was from a foreign country because my muttered words were indistinct. My vocabulary came from books, not conversation, so I mispronounced many words. In addition, my mother and father spoke with some archaic forms, like *warsh* for *wash*. I worried about how the spelling for *Washington Street*, where we lived, did not match our pronunciation, *Warshington*. For *root* we said *r-yuuh-t*, instead of *rute*. Instead of *yes*, we said, *yeow*. William Conrad, the radio actor for Matt Dillon on *Gunsmoke*, used the same pronunciation, but not many other people outside the family. I was self-conscious about speaking, so writing was a more reliable medium.

My parents gave me a children's illustrated encyclopedia one Christmas. I loved the entry about alphabets. I learned how the old-time Algonquin and Iroquois people living in the Northeast had glyphs embedded in wampum-beaded belts or etched on bark or stone. These are emblems that become active when spoken aloud. I read how scripts are magical as they travel through time, like the letter *M* deriving from the Egyptian hieroglyphic for "water." Glyphs train readers to look for multiple meanings, so they suggest literary complexity.

Words can ignite joy. When my older sister Mary read storybook fairy tales, sometimes I would sit transfixed for hours afterward and go over the illustrations, repeating scenes. Syllables can wind around images and create entrancing spectacles.

As a small child, I seined conversations for magic, but my family nearly had lost the ability to narrate anything more than episodes. A few times they joked, and once that terrified me more than any scolding. My mother said she had pulled a muscle in her leg. She laughed and said my father should take her to the backyard and shoot her like a horse. By then I knew what guns were, and death, and so I feared my mother would be killed. I could not understand why everyone else laughed. This was a rough humor that took getting used to, a version of "Indian humor."

Silence can be as hostile as thrown knives. Even as a child, I knew the difference between evasive chatter in our household and tense silence. I learned to plumb depths of meaning. "The postman is late," my mother could say, and "The milk needs to be used before it goes sour." These commonplaces could be a prelude to an explosion of her temper. Or not.

I watch how people tell their stories through sighs, sideways glances, pauses, and motions of their hands. These were like movements of wind on water—irregular intervals but always continuous. I learned how to write my own story, shape and edit it, improve it, and create performances on white sheets of paper that always listen to my voice. I built my own carapace to protect my words.

❖

Winter is the time for gambling. I shuffled a deck of cards as soon as I could hold them in my small hands. I learned sideways riffles, fancy cuts, and how to stand cards on end and tilt them like dominoes into a smooth river. My grandfather played Casino with me—the four-card game with Big Casino and Little Casino. He showed how each hand is a compelling skirmish, and no matter what the outcome, it has to end. The cards must be reshuffled and dealt out again.

Whether he was winning or losing, he demonstrated the trash talk that cardplayers use to intimidate each other. "Cut 'em thick, beat 'em quick," he said. It was like the chatter in baseball—"Hey, batter, batter." I loved the rhymes and repeated them for days. "Cut 'em thin, bound to win." It was a charm that improved my luck. This is how I learned poetry, not as ornament but as spells. By the time I was born, everyone except my oldest sister was tired of children's books, and so card playing was my first exposure to verse, training for my future as a poet. Words created real consequences. We played for money, and any magic boost was allowed.

I calculated points of winning cards, good arithmetic lessons, and learned how to lose and hide my disappointment. Pain washes away with the remix of the next hand. Always a new chance lies in the future. I learned to quit while I was ahead.

Cards have their own livery. Queens are beautiful women framed in ruffled, delicate ovals. The kings are remote rulers in square-pleated shirts. I mistrust jacks and how they can threaten, trade places, and ruin hands. They challenge the kings and sometimes win. But nowhere are there princess cards to match the jacks.

Jokers, with their harlequin patchwork and grotesque grins, remind me of European court life from fairy tales. Never are they direct help. They turn up unexpectedly in other people's hands and give them an unfair edge. Sometimes they appear in my own straight runs or flushes, upsetting plans. They fall on the floor or stick at the back of a drawer. For some games they are removed, so their mutability is physical as well as being mathematical interruptions. They are the tricksters, the random factor, patchwork yellow-and-black charlatans within the rows of reds suits paired with black.

In the old days winter games were training for children and serious occupation for adults. One Delaware game was *puim*, similar to poker but with sixty short marked reeds—red and black, like suits. The shift from sixty reeds to fifty-two playing cards must have been an easy transition. Dealers shuffled them, dealt, and then points were counted—not much different from all-night poker games in which my grandfather had some of his grandest triumphs and worst defeats.

My brother, a mentor in this art, taught me to read people's minds when gambling. He played cards with me for hours, and when he had an extremely good or bad hand, I could feel the energies that guided his strategies. The air became more charged, or the room felt flat. When he saw a straight heart flush in his cards and could not restrain his response, I knew. But despite my best efforts, by the end of the games, overall, he won. He was a kid himself, just six years older than me, but he was my teacher. Even while playing with a beginner sister, he used every opportunity to memorize odds for each play, and he became a skilled gambler.

Brother was smart and funny and patient, like my grandfather. He told me Grandfather was kindly, a grownup who played games with him when others would not take the time. But once, as a childish bravado, Brother ridiculed him in a card game. Grandfather would never play cards with him again. When he made a vow, he kept it.

Card games taught how chance is a genuine force, random but powerful. An offhand remark to an adult could be taken as an insult and cause unexpected loss. Dice, which seemed inanimate, could engage unseen powers, outside the logical workings of reason. Delawares had a dice game played with two-colored plum pits, *hubhub*, shaken in a basket. The black pits, or dice, connected to the cold winter of dark nights. Red- or white-colored dice were the summer and warmth. Today's casino businesses on reservations link to historic games of chance. In our frame houses with leaky windows and no insulation, the extremes of weather were vivid. We lived without air conditioning until the mid-1960s in the hot, dry plains, where 115 degrees is not uncommon. The binary of seasons paralleled the dice colors. Both cold and hot weather drove people to shelter, where gambling games passed the time. Tragedy and good fortune could strike unexpectedly at any time, like lightning, and both could disorder the daily routine.

I never knew if my grandfather gambled with dice, but when I grew up, my brother, who was close to him, always had playing dice in his room. Brother taught me to shake them in my cupped hands, concentrate, blow my breath on them, and throw. The concentration phase, a chance to alter the spin, was a mental challenge, the part where we could send messages to the cubes.

As I played these winter games, I saw numbers as individual characters. The sevens slink like cats, pause, and pose. They have an elegance. Elevens are difficult to count. Twelve dots create rows of eyes. The ones are solitary. Threes are "treys" and so have a slangy nickname and are friendly. Algebra came later, but this narrative was my first connection to numbers.

Dice with black, etched dots clacked with a satisfying sound. They were made of bone or ivory then, not plastic. We played, truly, a game of bones. This was during the polio years, when a boy my brother's age died a few blocks north of our neighborhood. Louise Erdrich writes about this serious side of chance when she describes charms of powerful Ojibwe gamblers: "Gamblers in the old days kept a powder of human bones—dried, crushed, pounded fine—to rub on their hands." Around us people died in blizzards, and summer tornadoes killed others. We heard stories of businessmen losing everything in one dice game. The random factor was a stark reality. When my siblings and I played dice, winning was serious business as we learned the odds of failure and the transience of success.

Besides dice and cards, my brother had dozens of miniature plastic toys, much more numerous than dolls. He launched platoons of World War II army soldiers; Crusaders with lances and broadswords; a few cowboys with neckerchiefs and lassos; and many Indians with drawn bows that could be pointed any direction. I wanted to have a box full of powerful fighters like he did. I stayed on his good side so I could watch him arrange fields of fighters and even hold a few.

Brother taught me to "Indian wrestle," starting from a position of locked legs, and how to lob knives at a wooden board. We played mumblety-peg when my mother was out of sight—a game of chicken in which one person throws a blade as close to the opponent's foot as possible, and the one who flinches loses. When our father was not around, my brother taught me to load and shoot the .22-caliber rifle. Weapons were summer entertainment, the red suit. Winter, noir, was when indoor games of cards filled our minds. We were just a few years from life-or-death Old West games of faro and high-stakes poker. My brother learned the spell of gambling from his grandfather, and he passed it down. The lineage went back as far as anyone could remember.

Today a bronze Kaw Indian man with drawn bow stands on top of the Kansas state capitol building, his arrow pointing at the North Star. The bowstring is taut. This is the first gesture in a story or the first card dealt in a hand. I want to be that figure. I want to shuffle and deal a new hand, in control of my fate. I want to stand at the statue's height and notch an arrow, draw the bow full length, and pierce the heart of the most remote winter star. I want to return to those early days, load the dice, and change my grandfather's luck.

❖

All of us kids in the neighborhood, girls or boys, played cowboys and Indians. We saw westerns at the movies and *Gunsmoke* on television. We brandished both chrome-plated six-shooters and bows and arrows. Western history was the backdrop for our games, and sometimes we had more vivid lessons.

When our Girl Scout troop went to the local museum, we saw a human skull with an embedded arrowhead. In those days human remains were often parts of exhibits, a practice now outlawed. The curator Mr. Soden, a man who looked like Doc on *Gunsmoke*, said it was skull of an Indian killed by another Indian. At the time, the 1950s, we were children, and the skull was creepy yet compelling. Mr. Soden said it came from Pawnee Rock, about two hundred miles farther west. As a child, I figured we could be warned in time if there were another raid by Pawnees. The possibility did not seem unrealistic to us children. Many of us had Native heritage, but none of us admitted to being Pawnee, fearsome fighters and not to be taken lightly. The violence of one Native man against another was a surprise, though, undercutting the cowboy and Indian oppositions on television. Another skull was a settler with an ax blade gash. Wood axes were important in the nineteenth century as tools and also could be makeshift weapons. This detail did not appear on popular television either.

We saw a Victrola with a wax cylinder, and as Mr. Soden played it for us, we heard Enrico Caruso's tenor murmur across the decades. This was in the basement of the Civic Auditorium, in a tiny room with small windows that admitted only snippets of light. The dim past was laid out in orderly rows of exhibits, like gravestones, and the semidarkness made the past even more similar to death.

In the basement-level tomb of history only the faintest sounds could be heard, like the distant cry of a tenor. Mr. Soden showed how the departed are far in the distance, behind us, and only a bit of indirect light sifts through dust motes to lighten the shadows. Yet under brick streets in this hidden room, the past could continue its momentum through bedrock.

When we played "guns" and chose sides, I picked the Indians, no question. We had a series of storybooks that I learned to read to myself. I followed a Lakota boy and girl on roan ponies through gorgeous grassy hillsides. I read this book series often, and the landscape attached to my imagination. It was the only book we had about the grasslands, where we lived. When the neighborhood kids chose up sides and counted who could have arrows and who could have rope lassos, I chose the arrows. I also chose cap guns. Why not both?

My grandfather grew up as both Native and a cowboy. As a boy, he helped his grandparents and uncles run cattle on their land. As long as Grandfather lived, he wore plaid flannel shirts, sometimes with pearl buttons. He kept his hair short at the neck, but his fine hair crested in a thick pompadour, like a rodeo star.

When I was small, I had some flannel shirts like Grandfather's. I let my hair grow as long as my mother would let me, and I tore out the prickly bobby pins. In summertime I tolerated pigtails and braids. For whatever reason my mother allowed my tendencies toward being a tomboy. I had a few fights as a kid and felt I could protect myself, especially after boxing lessons from my brother.

This is what people expected of women when I was growing up. Indeed, my mother often told me I needed to be prepared to take care of a family in any emergency. It was never a woman who died in her dire scenarios, always a man, so a woman had to be ready for many roles. We were cowboys and Indians, we were women, and sometimes, also, we were men.

❖

Today I remember the old people clearly, parents and grandparents. They described crystal radios made from wire wound around oatmeal boxes. My father's first radio was a marvel, and as he explained it, I could see the miracle of capturing radio waves out of the air and making them tangible. We had no television until I was twelve, so radio was our constant companion.

The dark plains around us were transformed into a friendly ocean of radio waves, especially at night, when most stations had signed off. In the grasslands, with few elevations, reception is most clear. In the 1950s and 1960s I remember broadcasts from New Orleans and Chicago. Hearing Jimmy Reed at 1:00 a.m. was life altering. Wichita radio stations played Charlie Parker and Louis Armstrong. They and other musicians traveled the railroad through Kansas and stopped to pick up extra cash. Local bands also wailed away in broadcasts but disappeared in morning light. In the unknown measures of prairie space, radio voices and distant grandparents all swirled together.

Music lessons were part of our childhood at a time when most families had pianos in the front rooms. Mexican American classmates played in musical groups for their community. African Americans and other classmates were in garage bands that sometimes produced professional musicians like Kelley Hunt and drummer Jack Mouse. I practiced scales on the piano but could not coordinate the layers of treble and bass notes. My father's clarinet was in a closet, so that one-note instrument became mine. After some years of practice I advanced enough to play in a local college jazz band, under mentorship of a long-suffering teacher, a bebop jazz musician, Larry Alderson. Music was a refuge for me at a time when words came with difficulty. I was so shy, I could hardly speak in most classes and then only awkwardly.

My classical music teacher presented one of the most important lessons of my life. This was Mr. Liegl, born in Vienna and a former clarinetist with the Minnesota Symphony. He berated me weekly for my lackluster performance. I knew he was justified. One lesson, as I played assigned pieces for him, he stopped me.

"*Pianissimo*," he said, "does not just mean low volume. The tone should be alive." He tapped the music stand with his wooden pointer, *fortissimo*. "*Pianissimo* means controlled passion, not absence of passion."

Something clicked. Nothing is empty, not even the spaces between sky and earth where nothing is visible. My emotional climate, also, is never neutral. Although I may be silent, my body feels a wide range of inner life. Silence has a meaning beyond void.

Once when my grandfather visited our family, a few years before he died, I awoke in the night, terrified, and turned on the lamp, waking everyone in the room. My grandfather said nothing, and I was ashamed of my childish fears. After a while, I turned off the lamp. We never spoke of this. I never understood until now where my fright came from—there was no dream, and I never again startled in the night like that. But I remember that sense of sudden jarring into consciousness. Unseen terrors could arise at any time as well as magical music riffs. That night I caught a ripple of fear. Perhaps it was an aftershock of the Gnadenhutten killings and other nighttime tragedies.

Grandfather did not seem surprised at my night panic. He did not complain, nor did he comfort me. My disturbance was a fact, like a dog twitching in its sleep. As I think back, this was the most chilling fact. We shared, in that unspoken exchange, the fact of terror. It is the text behind the stories, suspended in unrecorded oral histories of loss through the generations—massacres, plagues, accidents. Night's silence can be prelude to safety or loss.

❖

Like most people, I learned a one-word story of Native history in the Americas: "Defeat." Details of genocide were not in the elementary schoolbooks. Thirty-five of us children sat through history lessons at Walnut Elementary, fall semester, 1959. Baby boomer classes were overcrowded, with no time for questions.

We first studied Spanish explorers, then the Revolutionary War, then more pages devoted to settlers. Blue and green and red edges of the book arranged historic eras like dominoes. For the Civil War we learned how wilderness in the West was empty but also Indians—the book's term—inhabited it. I waited for the teacher to explain this paradox, but all I heard was Lewis and Clark were hero explorers. Davy Crockett killed Indians in Kentucky, so real civilization could advance. Almost half the students in that part of Kansas had Native heritage, but that fact was ignored except for a few times, when we were asked about our families.

The classroom had a large pastel wall map, and soon I realized the middle part of it, our lime-green part, had few famous people or battles. The textbook author did not know about Walnut Elementary or the Kansans or midwestern Indigenous people. We were phantoms.

My impression of school days history is not exaggerated, nor is it antiquated. One year ago, at a library discussion near my hometown, I heard audience members insist that the Great Plains region was empty before the nineteenth century. The same people, lifelong inhabitants of the region, find flint tools in their fields. Gardening in the center of a large town, I have uncovered pink flint tools made from stone mined in Iowa. Scrapers, knives, and points turn up along every stream bed between St. Louis and Denver. By the nineteenth century most arrows were tipped with metal, not flint, so these are several hundred years old, and some Ice Age points appear in local river rubble. Everywhere evidence of history is underfoot.

Burial mounds are common along midwestern valleys, despite destruction of the plow. I know the locations of several local mounds. Place names such as Kansas, Wakarusa, Neosho, Wichita, Topeka, and Shawnee label the landscape. Yet this reality is almost invisible in pioneer history.

I learned more European settler perspective through Saturday afternoon movies, attended by all of us neighborhood kids. In the 1950s Native people appeared as second-rate people who were sidekicks, never the real heroes. Tonto accompanied the Lone Ranger but made no arrests. "Good Indians" were helpful Squanto types; "bad Indians" fell off horses into oblivion.

In John Wayne movies some Native audiences can understand the insults of Lakota and Navajo actors as they create dialogue in their own languages. "You smell like dog excrement!" says the stoic Indian guide to John Wayne in Lakota. "*Wasicu*, you greedy hoarder, go that way to roll in more of it!" he says as the parley ends and the Duke saddles up. "Yah-Ta-Hey!" says John Wayne, as he waves good-bye, which is poorly accented Navajo for "hello." These jokes are some small revenge for the indignities of Hollywood westerns.

We kids imitated Matt Dillon's drawl, Maverick's jokes, and Paladin's slit-eyed glare. On the playground, unlike real life, odds were even. We all had noisy cap guns and arrows made from stripped willow branches. In southeastern Kansas, former Indian Territory, many of our neighbors descended from Oklahoma tribal members who had fought against the Confederates and fled to Kansas during the Civil War. I heard Cherokee and Creek words at recess, mostly exclamations: *Gaaaw!* and *Ooo-weee!* Native history was woven into our lives, but we had few ways, as children, to understand how.

In high school history we learned a few one-sided details. For the Trail of Tears story we heard that Indians had ruined farmland and had to be removed. In our text we did not see a portrait of Sequoyah with the Cherokee syllabary. We did not see murdered families at Horseshoe Bend.

I learned of the Cherokee Trail of Tears from a high school friend, Cathryn. Her grandmother had walked from Georgia to Oklahoma. This was real history, not a lesson of dates and battles from the textbook. "Grandma told how soldiers beat them and raped the women," she said. We were old enough to understand, and I sat horrified. She continued, "They shot anyone who fell behind, even pregnant women." As she spoke, Cathryn used the term *Grandma* as though this were her own grandmother's story. Only later did I realize the story had been handed down through the generations, and it would have been a great-grandmother four or five generations back. Her words had immediacy, and so this blonde, blue-eyed classmate helped me realize how experience is the defining identity of an Indigenous person. Her oral stories defined her, stories she had learned at her grandmother's knee.

As long as a people remember, my Cherokee friend taught me, they are not conquered. In time I learned my own family's connection to Cherokee traditions, on my father's side. My parents

downplayed their family history, but many of my classmates kept
alive the stories from their own Native families. They helped me
understand the continuity of community from pre-reservation times
into the future.

❖

Grandfather leaves behind gifts. His lifetime is a lesson. He remained
silent about his spiritual beliefs, and so he avoided conflict. That was
one teaching. As other relatives insisted they had absolute truths,
he remained silent, a form of tolerance. He was no evangelist.

Another teaching is physical health. He had good basic health
until he became ill with lung cancer, in his seventies—a goodly
life span in those days. He smoked cigarettes but before they were
understood to be a health hazard. He ate with relish but moder-
ately. With coffee, he dipped doughnuts or cookies, to sweeten the
dark brew. He did not turn down food, but he did not take second
helpings. He lived through all the stages of life: childhood, youth,
adulthood, and old age.

Every Christmas an enormous box of chocolate candies arrived
from him and Grandmother, and on Christmas Day we children
rustled through the brown tissues for coconut haystacks, caramels,
chocolate-covered cherries, and truffles. The lesson of sweetness is
an easy one to learn.

One Christmas it was my turn to purchase Grandfather a gift.
At eleven years old I saved my allowance and poker earnings dili-
gently for Christmas expenses. My mother added a few dollars to
the sum. It was a mild December Saturday, and downtown was
filled with ranchers from outside of town as well as neighbors. My
family went to a large clothing store, and I wandered through the
aisles of the men's department. Because it was an overcast day, the
indoors was deep in shadows. The wooden floorboards under my
feet were as dark as wet tree bark. I knew I was in foreign country,
especially when I saw a rough-looking cowboy in a ten-gallon hat
standing by the aftershave gift boxes.

As I looked over shelves, I tried to imagine what my elderly

24. Denise (Dotson) Low, age nineteen. Photograph taken in Emporia, Kansas, 1968, by Bruce Balkenhol, family friend.

grandfather would want for Christmas. Certainly not toys. Even then, I understood he was poor, so I wanted to make the dollars count. The pearl button cowboy shirts, with matching handkerchiefs, enticed me, but they cost too much—eight dollars. Eventually, I settled on a brown tie with stud. It would match his eyes.

My mother reviewed my choice without comment. I sighed with relief. Since she was not critical, it must be acceptable. "Don't lose it," she finally said. "You need to wrap it in time for the mailman."

Now I wonder at my mother's restraint as she left me on my own to solve this problem. She was teaching me the importance of gifts, as my grandfather once had taught her. And this is the way of Native parents—letting children make their own decisions, whether good or bad. She showed me how consequence is the best teacher.

I never knew how Grandfather received my gift, but that did not matter. He was there, he was alive during my childhood, and he was my grandfather. I sent the gift, and this demonstrated that my grandfather was important.

Grandfather gave me another gift, one I did not recognize at the time—a red-and-black wool blanket. My mother had several blankets in our unheated upstairs room, where we talked, played cards, and watched television together. In the winter we used these blankets, which had come from Grandfather. When I left for college, my mother let me choose one, the red-and-black, to take with me. My mother always called it a "Mexican" blanket, yet I never saw that simple pattern before or since among Mexican textiles. It was scratchy wool, not cotton. I remember its fringes, the warp ends wound and tightly twisted, and the even lines of wool yarn. I used it for decades before it fell apart. The vermillion red and ink black colors never faded. When I slept at night, I had the warmth of my family, especially my grandfather, laid over me, even when I was far from home.

The linkage of child to parent is formed of many gifts—the strands of DNA as well as gifts of teachings. A simple blanket also is a daily gift, as it lends emotional as well as physical shelter.

❖

In my hometown youngsters roamed widely with no fear. Alleys, other people's backyards, or construction sites—kids free-ranged everywhere. Land was cheap, and suburban lots were half-acres, with mown lawns in front and tangled underbrush in back that crossed property lines. At the time I almost believed school social studies texts that presented Kansas as two-dimensional wheat fields. Yet at the edge of town, streets dipped and rose to sharp-edged ridges. Winding side streets named "Terrace" led toward sharp drops to teeming creeks. This was almost the same surroundings as my grandfather's hometown of Burns, which lies west eighty miles on Highway 50. As I grew up in this natural playground, my experiences were not unlike those of my grandfather when he was young.

I remember especially a neighbor's vacant lot of unplowed tallgrass prairie. This one perimeter—of giant bluestem, pokeberries, sunflowers, and a huge Osage orange tree—is my origination point as an adult. Lost within city limits, the rectangle of unbroken sod was a window into another dimension.

This new awareness began one afternoon when I was about eleven, as I cut across the neighbor's yard, through the alley, and past an old garage edged with damp earth. Shale broke into layers in the muddy pathway, and between the layers were delicate images of ferns. Here I tarried. The impressions were fresh, as though made yesterday, and so the rock's history seemed near at hand. I may have collected a sample, or maybe only my sight collected the images for this memory. Eventually, I roused.

On past an old well I crossed an abandoned rose garden and then arrived at a city lot, probably fifty feet by seventy feet. Like Alice in Wonderland gone into a rabbit hole, I stopped in my tracks before a six-feet-tall wall of big bluestem grass. It was late summer, and grasshoppers buzzed about the stems. Dragonflies busy themselves this time of year as they migrate. Prisms flashed from their wings. This lot somewhat resembled my mother's unweeded strawberry patch but on a much grander scale. I had read Conan books by Robert E. Howard and relished how he evoked bizarre civilizations. Howard's citadels were not unlike the stumbling old houses on country roads around town. And here this unique stretch of grass, with broken brickwork at one end and old vines at the other, seemed exotic.

At that age I was no longer a small child and not yet a teenager.

I was alone but not abandoned, teetering at the edge of decision. I experienced a sense of eternal time. Poet William Stafford describes this sense, which he felt after camping along the Cimarron River in Kansas: "No person was anywhere, nothing, just space, the solid earth. . . . That encounter with the size and serenity of the earth and its neighbors in the sky has never left me." Stafford also records how this one experience initiated a lifelong quest. His childhood experience wends through his writings, not as nostalgia but, rather, as imagery that evokes the ongoing experience of childhood. His writings do not recall the past; they nurture its continuing presence.

On that fateful afternoon I considered the invisible tether to my mother. She was cross as a bear if I strayed too far. I knew I was within earshot of her, so I could hear her call for dinner, but I was far beyond her sight. The squared realm of towering wildlife was irresistible, and so I plunged in. Like Stafford, I entered and never left.

During the next weeks I did not notice how solitary I had become, but I was never lonely. Once I took my sister, but she soon became bored and left. But as I trampled grass and counted pokeberry spikes, I became aware that two older women in the next-door house watched. It was a brown-shingled bulwark, a wooden ship stranded in the grassy shallows. Now I understand how, as they sat by their window, they were enjoying the novelty of a child absorbed in play, like a species of animal. That bit of natural space was also theirs. My memory of passing time there now entwines with images of those women, so that I see myself from their window. Their presence foreshadowed my adult self, and I was their past childhoods. We mirrored each other, like paintings are yet another facet of past and present time.

At first I ignored the couple's presence, but finally they greeted me and warned me away from their garden pond, just off the path, in case I might drown. The shallow pool of scalloped lily pads was a temptation, but I kept my distance as instructed. Another time the women asked me indoors to see their African violets. They took me down root cellar steps to a primitive basement with dirt floor. There, glow lights illumined an indoor garden, organized in neat rows. The pale-blue, fuchsia, cerise, lilac, lavender, ivory, and baby-pink blossoms were an amazing discovery in the midst of a drab drought.

Grass outside grew in whorls according to a seasonal calendar, and the women cultivated their potted garden according to human design. The natural world was not at odds with their view but, rather, another aspect of it. As Native peoples organized the Flint Hills into hunting parks with fire, so these women entered into a partnership with the plant world. Their engagement in aesthetics—the lily pond, the violets, and their ordered parlor furniture—prepared me for experiencing natural order in language. The cultivated African violets were one view; the unplowed lot of bluestem grass was another. Neither excluded the other.

As the days went on, I learned how an undomesticated space did not privilege humans. Snake holes in the grass and their papery, scaled skins gave evidence of co-inhabitants. Red squirrels and rabbits came near me when I was still. I observed how my own form has a bisymmetry similar to mammals, a capacity for motion and rest, and digits. I wished for a tail. As I learned about different beings in this outward space, our commonalities became clear. Each night we all seek shelter from the four winds.

During another visit with the old women, in that tomblike basement smelling of potting soil, we talked about death. As a youngster, my notion of the afterlife was a biblical punishment for accidents or polio. Yet they told me death was beautiful—a part of the cycles. I did not believe them, but I later found a desiccated squirrel corpse and looked at the ingenious workings of its skeleton, rather than throwing it away.

Becoming old was the lesson I learned, in all its forms—old age for the women, late summer, and the full-blown Osage orange tree with thorns. An ancient box turtle trudged through the grassy aisles one of these days, dusty and weary looking, and I marveled at it as a living fossil. The elderly women were substitute grandparents. Grandfather Bruner was still alive at that time, connected by the same hot winds that blow continuously from the west, all summer and into September, but I seldom saw him.

As I recall that summer, I conjure the women again and bring them back into existence. I recall when I first entered their sight, beyond glass panes, near the end of their earthly lives. Then I was living within a make-believe world, barely differentiated from the life around me. As a child, I walked into that expanse of unlimited waving fronds, and then I crossed the line into the realm of those old women. I now observe nature more than participate as a natural being.

I enter my own house now and sit in a stuffed chair covered by doilies. I describe that child in the grassy lot as though she were someone else. This story of my grandfather and my mother has become my own, as my past grows longer than my future.

❖

My mother instilled in me a fear of capture. In our small town she watched over me like a hawk. One of my greatest forbidden actions was to roam beyond earshot. This hypervigilance was out of proportion for our midwestern town, where few crimes occurred. Parents kept an eye on all the neighborhood children as they wandered. We roamed with dogs at our heels, on foot, on bikes, and occasionally on horseback. Within a several-mile span we were safe, but my mother never relaxed. Unspeakable fears were the most powerful forces in her life, even though she could not explain them. She just warned: "Gypsies will get you. I could never forgive myself."

"Gypsies" hardly appeared in our part of Kansas—I never saw any, ever. A few Gypsy, or Roma, groups traveled two-lane highways to the north on their way to other parts of the country, but the Kansas grasslands were no regular destination.

Nonetheless, my mother kept before us the imminent possibility of kidnapping. This apprehension echoes the real loss of Native children to boarding schools. I have a Navajo friend whose grandmother held a shotgun on social workers when they tried to remove children from the home. The year was 1985. During the

1950s and before, indeed, many Native children were taken from their homes by the government. In 1871 the United States Congress passed a law, the Indian Appropriations Act, which made Native people wards of the state. Children could be taken from their homes and forced to attend distant boarding school. That may have been the event that caused my great-great-grandparents, in Ohio and in New Jersey, to leave everything and go west. Within a few years after this law was passed, they all made the move. My mother's parents and grandparents had avoided boarding schools by hiding their identity, but fear of losing children still existed as a reflex.

I have talked with hundreds of Native people whose childhoods were cut short when government boarding school officials captured them, cut their hair, and forced them to attend church and schools. Many experienced physical and sexual abuse. Ramapough Mountain Indians of New Jersey, a Delaware community, emphasize the peril of their children on their website: "Upon hearing that a parent had died, or become ill, so called do-gooders would rush into the mountains and gather up the children, and take them away. Some never had contact with their relatives again." The official websites of most Indigenous nations usually have community consensus before posting and are reliable sources.

This Ramapough story is but one of many about how tribal groups faced continued efforts to terminate their communities. My grandfather's paternal grandparents came from this northeastern region, almost forgotten until Connecticut's Mohegans reemerged and built a casino.

Joseph Bruchac, of Abenaki heritage, tells of Algonquin communities who survive in upstate New York, Vermont, New Hampshire, and Maine. He told me his story of Gypsy, or rather Abenaki, persecution in 1984, and later he published a book with more explanation. I have never forgotten his chilling story. His people lived in a traditional Native settlement on Lake Champlain, near the Canadian border. Their unaffiliated Abenaki group practiced subsistence living until attacked by a mob of townspeople.

They lived in longhouses and wigwoms (wigwom is the Abenaki word for "house") and existed by hunting, fishing, and trading for a few material goods. One night, however, the decision was made by some town fathers to get rid of the "gypsies", who were aliens and might even be German sympathizers and were not to be trusted because they went back and forth between there and Canada. They came down on the Abenaki village with armed men and trucks, loaded the adults into the trucks, and gave the children up for adoption. The trucks roared out of town, and no one knows for sure what happened to those people.

Rather than admit Algonquin Indigenous people still lived on their aboriginal land, which might suggest legal ownership, the mob used the term *Gypsy*.

These northern Algonquins were kin to the Bruners' New Jersey Delaware people, and the common theme is danger. Identities were hidden to avoid violence. Onondaga elder Mitchell Bush worked in the 1960s to 1980s as a Bureau of Indian Affairs tribal enrollment director, and he remembers the Ramapough Lenapes. He knew a Delaware man from there named Bruner in the 1950s who lived at Haskell Institute while he attended the University of Kansas. Billy Mills, the Olympic runner, and other Native people lodged at Haskell to avoid discrimination. Bush verified this Bruner man was a New Jersey Delaware, but at the university he told no one.

I never met Roma people when I was growing up. However, I remember an unknown family settled into a house on Emporia's main street when I was sixteen. They set up signs offering "Gypsy" palm readings and fortune-telling. One afternoon I took five dollars and ventured across the sidewalk for a palm reading. A woman in a long, tiered dress took me to a back room, collected the money, and looked at my hand. She said I would have a troubled love life, and I did not doubt her. She said I had good health, a fact that anyone could observe. Then she ended by saying, "Your family has secrets." Perhaps every family has secrets. The reading did not make me a convert to occult beliefs.

Afterward her extended family of children and adults were still in the front room. As I left, I asked where they came from. The fortune-teller explained they were Apaches from New Mexico, and the men worked for the Santa Fe railroad, as a track repair crew. They just called themselves "Gypsies" so they could get along in towns. Being a Gypsy was preferable to being an Indian. Sometime during the next winter they left town, and I cannot imagine that they had an easy existence in the 1960s, either as Apaches or Gypsies.

❖

Once an Eastern Cherokee filmmaker interviewed me about Grandfather's Delaware identity. Under four-dimensional lights footage would show invisible hands over my mouth trying to muffle utterance. They would be my parents' hands, powerful even after death. My tongue went dry as I tried to formulate meaning from experiences buried within a cache of denied stories. I rasped. Finally, I croaked brief answers to the interviewer. That flawed footage no doubt was discarded, but it helped me identify a point of pain that needed tending. It helped me begin to claim my own story and that of my family.

Other times I have struggled to speak in front of people about my family's past. One Veteran's Day at Haskell Indian Nations University, a group of us met at the campus gazebo to commemorate the day, led by Ketoowah leader Benny Smith. Elders offered prayers. I was alone and orphaned—my parents gone to the next world by then. At my turn to speak I pulled into my shell and could not name my grandfather as a Delaware or a veteran. I held back as others described battles in Korea and Vietnam and then stories about the world wars and Native wars of resistance. These were Cherokee and Kiowa and Ponca people, from many different families.

By their example I learned how much I had lost. These tribal members, despite assimilationist policies, knew their history. They could recite hundreds of years of events. Their tacit encouragement led me to question my remaining family elders. This was years ago, but they, like my grandfather, were correct about how each individual has a responsibility to a larger history.

A few years later my older brother told me easily, when I asked— "Yes, Grandfather was Indian." Everyone knew it. Brother had no hesitation, no chokehold on his throat.

My older sister Mary also knew our grandfather's identity but never thought it was important. She left home as soon as she could, taking a ruler and measuring which coast was farthest from our address. She followed a pencil-drawn latitude west to the Pacific. Such was the geography of distance in our family. She lived out her life among palm trees, blue lilies of the Nile, and crows—always a small group of the noisy birds in her garden. She kept dogs underfoot, her own pack of small wolves. She listened to her dreams carefully and sometimes talked with me to help unravel their meaning. Reading books and reading signs around her were the family heritage.

We siblings loved each other and counted on each other. I suffered the tragedy of being born the youngest, so I soon learned how quickly families can break apart.

First, my sister Mary left home when I was ten. I remember my grandmother weeping that Christmas, as it would be the last we would all be together. Mary returned only twice after that, in fifty years. Our brother left home as soon as he could, at seventeen years of age, and that loss continues to be one of my worst experiences. When I was a vulnerable fifteen-year-old, my last sibling, my sister Jane, left for California to take advantage of a scholarship to Stanford University. I was devastated. I worried I would hardly ever see her again, like my mother hardly saw her only brother.

After that my parents hung onto me, their youngest, and my will to leave weakened. I learned how to be distant within myself, so geography was not necessary for departure. When speaking with them, I learned to avoid difficult subjects, and by my adulthood I knew all the sore points. Repressed speech was my habit more than ever.

❖

My twenty-five-plus years of teaching at Haskell Indian Nations University, formerly Haskell Institute, gave me daily contact with people from many Indigenous nations. Within weeks of starting to work at this all-Native federal school in 1984, I felt comfortable on its grounds. The best part was the storytelling. I have been fortunate to hear Native stories, histories, cosmologies, jokes, powwow tunes, drumming, funeral orations, ceremonies, confrontations, prayers, gossip, and lectures. Spoken words carry much spirit.

Because of rigid federal rules at Haskell regarding tribal membership, "Indian preference" laws, I was on the outside in a new way. Yet I knew how to listen, so I had a niche as a quieter member of the Haskell family. Grandfather's example taught me useful lessons for getting along at Haskell.

Haskell is at a crossroads in Indian Country, and through the years I saw most of the leading figures—Sherman Alexie, Paula Gunn Allen, Thomas Banyanca, Jim Barnes, Clyde Bellecourt, Kimberly Blaeser, Allison Hedge Coke, Vine Deloria Jr., Heid Erdrich, Lee Francis III, Lee Francis IV, Joy Harjo, Geary Hobson, Clara Sue Kidwell, Wilma Mankiller, Russell Means, William Mehojah, N. Scott Momaday, Simon Ortiz, Carter Revard, Buffy Saint-Marie, Joan Shenandoah, Benny Smith, Crosslin Smith, Wes Studi, Luci Tapahonso, John Trudell, Ophelia Zepeda, and many more. All presented living examples of how the past folds into present and future time frames. One elder told us how important faculty were to students, as stand-ins for relatives. This teaching stayed with me.

Two moments stand out among the maelstrom of years. One is the arrival of elderly Athabaskan dancers at a powwow. They traveled a long distance from Alaska, and many had not been outside home villages. It was August, and the drone of locusts was constant. One of them asked, "What is that noise?"

"What noise? I hear nothing," responded a local student. Finally, someone recognized the low-level buzz that fills the air in late August, what no one else separated from the daily breeze. The insects were exotic to the Alaskans and disturbing.

Also, they had not experienced lightning. In the far North electric storms do not occur. During their presentation storm clouds gathered with sheet lightning. An elder went to the microphone. "We are amazed at this sign from the clouds," she said. "We have no thunder or lightning, just rain and snow." Then they proceeded to dance, about two hours, without stopping in the sultry heat. They had come this far, and despite their brief slot in the program, they felt they should present their best. This was not a powwow dance for entertainment. It was a prayer for the world.

A second moment I remember is when a Cree spiritual leader arrived from Montana. He was brought to find a missing person. We sat with him in a room as he told his story, about losing his wife and young children in a car wreck. He despaired. Yet, he said, such loss is what precedes spiritual gifts. This was part of his past and important for how he became able to help people. As he explained this, I understood that the missing man was dead, but no one said this out loud. Then, after blessings and smoke purifications, he asked the women to leave the room because the next part was men's spirituality. From this I understood gender in a new way. I appreciated my womanhood as unique, even with many cross-gender activities in my experience.

After time at Haskell I turned to stories from my own background and questioned my parents. I also noticed what was omitted, and this said as much as their assertions. Mother was the crucial generational link to Grandfather's life. She had lost so many stories. My mother told only a few anecdotes about her close friend Ada, a Native from Oklahoma who was like my aunt. Mother told only brief outlines of her grandparents' and parents' lives. The term *sui generis* describes her—she believed she was one of a kind, unlike anyone before or after her. This shortsightedness saved her from learning overwhelming stories of loss. It also left her adrift in her own isolation. I did not want to be like her.

My mixed heritage is not easy. Geary Hobson, a professor and storyteller who came to Haskell to speak, gives me courage, especially with his account about his early forebear Alexis Pierre Beatte, a mixed-blood man of Quapaw and French ancestry. Catlin would not paint his portrait because, even in the 1830s, stereotypes of Indian appearance were set. Geary still refuses to accept this void as he writes narratives for journals and books.

Years ago I was in Utah presenting poetry, and a man from Georgia stopped me at a restaurant. He had heard my presentation and knew I was teaching at Haskell. "You are Indian," he said.

"No, I'm not enrolled in a tribe," I responded.

"That doesn't matter. Your folks still were Indian. They went through the hard times."

Then he explained he was from an isolate Cherokee group in Georgia that managed to avoid the Trail of Tears. He persisted in his tale, and then he gave me an essay he had written about the psychological stress on people who do not look like stereotypical Indians yet live in the aftermath of the same history. The discord between appearance and identity creates inner turmoil, according to his research. It was the first time I had considered this idea and also the intergenerational effects of trauma. It was also one of the first times someone had looked at me and identified me as a Native person.

I kept the man's paper and read it several times, feeling sorry for him. The last reading I felt sorry for myself. I showed the paper to Haskell students who struggled with identity, and I learned from it myself. This was a step toward reclaiming my family's history.

❖

As I age, more aspects of the spirit world braid into my life. I remember my mother's eyes became portals within her ancient lids. She lived to be almost ninety. I expect to make a hundred, and one day I will peer at the world through such eyes.

My dead mother's spirit follows me. Sometimes she is in the kitchen during meals. A whirlwind of unvoiced words circles her place at the table. My older departed sister sits next to her in the straight-backed chair. If I pour coffee and set out a cigarette, my Delaware grandfather arrives with a blessing. Tobacco can carry messages to him.

I worry about growing old not because of infirmities but because more and more departed relatives crowd around the kitchen table. Many of my Menominee husband's older relatives have also joined the spirits, and they signal to us as well. Maybe it is easier to have Christian relatives who wait quietly in underground coffins for the celestial city of Jerusalem, a place beyond my responsibility. Whoever sits at the table must be tended.

This is not a world of consistent, logical uniformity. Laguna Pueblo writer Leslie Marmon Silko explains irrationality as a dimension of physical laws, "where the gravity is either weaker or stronger, where even light may speed up or slow down." So, perhaps my departed relatives breathe quicker light rather than air and their weight is barely perceptible. Time is a circle of gravity, light, and matter. We incarnate. We disperse into light, all in the medium of time, but we do not disappear.

Here, if you can see him sitting next to me, you can meet my grandfather. We can see him start to smile. He may be a vortex of silence to others, long buried in a country cemetery, but to me he speaks.

❖

A Native friend made a suicide attempt yesterday, and I spent time talking with him. American Indigenous people have a much higher suicide rate than any other United States population. He was not a statistic, though, as I stood by his hospital bed. What encouragement is there for a young diabetic man in poor health to help him endure the painful experience of that disease? I took a deep breath and told him he must live for the next generation. Children, nieces, and nephews all depend on him. He cannot start a cycle of self-violence. He cannot abandon a daughter with the example of suicide as a viable option. I described Grandfather Bruner and his difficult and heroic life as a survivor. As an adult, I see his life in larger terms.

Grandfather lost two of his four children, had a bad injury, faced discrimination, and yet he kept going. He did not have a perfect life, but he endured. In his last photograph, on the wall behind him I see how he displayed two Santa Fe calendar prints—a Pueblo eagle dancer and a silversmith. The month is December, his birth month, and the dancer spreads wings above the numbers. He loved beauty. He also enjoyed a good laugh. When I have bad times, I remember his example of survival. I think of my children.

As we talked, I told my friend how the departed are not gone. Every day I remember my mother, the way she kept her muddy garden shoes by the back door. Or I use her cake pan. Or I hear her voice in the timbre of my own. I remember her stories of her father's kindness to her as he taught her proper manners. All of his lessons come down to me, in her attempts to describe her father. All of my friend's lessons will go through his children to the generations to come.

Once, when I was a young woman, a Native elder told me that younger people are always watching me, to see how to behave. Even though I was a mother by then, I had not understood that responsibility—not just for my own children but for all those who follow in the sequence of time. Since that lesson, I have tried to remember all the younger people who observe my example. I consider the seven generations ahead of me. I preserve the memory of seven generations behind, so I will know their history and have the power of self-knowledge. My grandfather's lessons continue into the twenty-first century.

PART 4

Today

Living in Delaware Country

The Kaw River rims the sky north of my home. It rises in the Smoky Hills of Kansas east of Penokee Man, curves through Lawrence, and empties into the Missouri River at Kansas City. In the early years the Delaware "outlet" to the plains for hunting trips stretched along this entire course. The river, usually called the Kansas River, is a daily reminder of a time when the north section of my town was officially Delaware territory, from 1829 to 1867. Many Delaware descendants, like me, still live in the former Delaware towns along this muddy waterway.

One moody November day, clouds a marbled gray, my husband and I travel the river to look for former Delaware trading posts. Without sun, dawn to noon to twilight will be the same hue. The dull light creates a timeless mood as we peer at the antiquated map and plot a course.

We drive through the Lawrence downtown, where we see visible history. Kansas was the eye of the storm over slavery, and some results of this conflict are frozen in architecture. Missouri ruffians burned Lawrence twice. The few surviving buildings from Quantrill's Raid are venerated landmarks. Because of effective preservationists,

25. Diminished Delaware Reserve, Leavenworth and Wyandotte Counties, in
northeastern Kansas, with Kansas River boundary on the south. Created by R. P.
Studley & Co., between 1850 and 1859. Used with permission of kansasmemory
.org, Kansas State Historical Society. Item no. 305064. Call no. R G4202 N63:2
D4 Z1850 .S8. KSHS Identifier: DART ID: 305064.

many other historic buildings remain as well. The old opera hall has
Gilded Age glamour. Turrets and cupolas ornament the vernacular
limestone courthouse. New buildings must blend designs with the
old styles, according to the city code. The result is an homage to
the town's noble past.

We cross the Kaw River to North Lawrence. Beyond the visitor's
center, a former Union Pacific Railroad depot, the change is immediate. Economy is the first rule of this adjunct town's appearance.
The few commercial buildings are utilitarian. Houses are old and
occasionally remodeled but often not. When we turn off the main
road, the settlement is strung out along bottomlands, small houses
dwarfed by large garden plots. Many are well kept, and many are
not. Nothing suggests the past history of Delaware lands.

I am surprised to find that any Delaware-era buildings survive.

26. Old Delaware Trading Post, North Lawrence, Kansas, 2014. Author's collection.

They are not protected by building codes, and so alterations make them almost invisible. A resident, Daniel Bentley, gave me the address of the Delaware trading post, on a road once called "Delaware Street." We follow newly numbered streets to the site.

The house is similar to most other buildings. Renovation is evident, but when we look more closely, the integrity of the original two-story form is preserved—a hall and parlor house with an overhang porch. The basic rectangular box has a porch of awning and posts and then various lean-tos jumbled at angles. According to a nineteenth-century historian, this basic cabin is an archaic Native form as well as European: "rectangular in ground-plan, and . . . constructed with a gable like a modern wall-tent, but with a hole in the top to let out the smoke." Inside this two-story model a staircase would divide the downstairs into two halves and lead upstairs to the same arrangement on the top floor. My house today, a California ranch-style house, also is a long rectangle with one front door and a medium-pitched roof for rain. This is a practical design for the climate. Materials differ, but the same compact structure continues to work well.

We stop at the next-door house to visit Bentley. His land would have been the post's cornfield, and he raises a large garden in the rich soil. He greets us at his door and comes outside to point out details of the original store.

"The north lean-to was once a kitchen," he says. "They cooked outdoors during the summer, on the north side for shade. I find kitchen things when I'm tilling the garden—shards of glass so old they have turned violet."

"Anything more unusual?" I ask. Antique glass is found at most old sites.

"A round metal spoon, very worn," he says, "with an unusually deep bowl."

"That sounds like Delawares. They used deep-bowled spoons, originally wood or copper," I say. "The shape is what would be Native, different from manufactured tableware."

"That must be it," he says.

We talk more about some other finds, including some arrowheads, but these were probably from earlier people. Knives, arrow points, scrapers, fish hooks, awls, and needles most often were made of metal by the mid-1800s. The detritus of a Delaware house site is almost identical to goods left around European American settler homes. An 1867 collection of Lakota and Cheyenne artifacts from a tipi encampment near Fort Larned, Kansas, displays a dozen coffee grinders, metal arrow points, bullet molds, and buttons. Military records of what historians call "Hancock's War" help date these captured items, which are remarkable for the dominance of trade items.

We thank Bentley for his help with local history. His neighbors kept alive memory of the Delawares in the oral tradition, even after the city changed street names.

The North Lawrence trading post dates to pre–Civil War times, when Delawares prospered. The Civil War as a terrible time for Delaware people. Most of them sided with the United States government, and the cost for their service was the Kansas land. While Delaware men fought in the Indian Home Guards, neighbors burned their buildings and stole livestock. A record by a government agent for the Delawares, Fielding Johnson, itemizes the theft of three hundred horses, pigs, and cattle from October to December 1862. Arson was another weapon, and the marauders' fires echoed terrorist tactics of Ohio and Pennsylvania. This intimidation forced Delawares to plan yet another move to the next Indian Territory, Oklahoma.

Deeds show the transfer of Delaware land to the railroads and wealthy farmers in the late 1860s. The bare bones of the story are in a local history:

> In a treaty between the United States and the Delaware Indians, ratified on August 22, 1860, the government granted to Sarcoxie, Chief of the Turtle Band, approximately 320 acres including the greater part of the site of North Lawrence. All of this land was transferred to Charles Robinson, Robert S. Stevens, and William A. Simpson by Sarcoxie and War-me-mar-o-qua, his wife, on November 2, 1861. Almost immediately afterwards, the tract was broken up by the transfer of a strip of land to the Eastern Division of the Kansas Pacific Railroad Company, and other smaller sales to settlers who had moved to the community.

Sarcoxie received and then sold North Lawrence land as the Turtle Band of Delawares faced overwhelming threats. One of the buyers, Robinson, was first governor of Kansas and a heroic abolitionist, yet he engineered this slick appropriation of the Delaware farmlands. One oral tradition story indicates he used the lumber from the Delaware religious building for his barn. The Delaware "big house" was on Robinson's holdings.

Kansas Delawares of the area keep alive their heritage, but few people outside their circle know they exist. In Lawrence almost no Delaware history appears in museums or on websites, yet they were

Civil War heroes. Military records of the Indian Home Guards show that "of a total of 201 eligible Delaware males between the ages of 18 and 45, 170 volunteered for service in 1862." Their efforts did not create allies among power brokers of the Kansas Territory, and reviving that history creates a conflicted view of the town fathers.

We are grateful to find this one building still standing. We thank Bentley and continue our trip.

We drive out of the maze of North Lawrence and turn east at Teepee Junction, a regional landmark. A former coach at Haskell Institute, Frank W. McDonald, built the fifty-feet-tall concrete tipi in 1928. He hired Navajo artist Tom Nokie to paint it with Plains Indian figures in headdresses. The odd American Indian–looking structure, a roadside attraction for years, was originally a gas station and beer garden. It was often staffed by the Haskell boarding school students for no pay. This is one of the few indications of a Native history, and it is for tourists. Nothing about it suggests an accurate history of Delaware people.

In the car I return to the old map, which shows the string of railroad stations named after Delaware leaders: Fall Leaf, Journey Cake (now Linwood), Lenape, Tiblow (Bonner Springs), and Secondine. Steamboats navigated the Kaw and stopped along the river at these towns in the 1830s. Railroads later used the same stops. They constructed bridges just low enough to block steamboat traffic, which ended their competition. The low trestles attest to the ruthlessness of that industry.

Along the way we see much farmland, and my husband mentions this is one of the best soils in the world, according to his geology class in college. The Rockies blew loess across the region, and a glacier from the Ice Age carried in more layers of soil. We see mostly fields of milo and corn but also many grand new houses. This is a mixed rural setting of gentrified and older places. All have a million-dollar view of rolling wooded hills and meadows.

We continue eastward to a collection of houses on Fall Leaf Road. On a bluff overlooking the river, we see a substantial brick building, which turns out to be an old schoolhouse. Local history sources date this building after the 1903 flood. When the old site of the town flooded, all the original buildings were lost, including any Delaware structures. Two huge black dogs appear, barking furiously, to hurry us on our way.

In Linwood, farther down the road, I think of my friend Janet Allen, who descends from the Delaware man Journey Cake. The town no longer bears his name, but the school district has a short history: "This brave man escaped his captors and journeyed a long distance home to the Linwood area. Along the way, he suffered many hardships, with only a small cake of corn bread for sustenance. He was re-christened 'Journey Cake' by his tribe after telling them his story upon his arrival home." This was the last leader before removal to Oklahoma. The town also had the name "Stranger," and the nearby creek bears this name. Settlers changed the town name to Linwood for the linden trees on the site. This also removed reminders of the Delaware presence.

A member from the Kansas Delaware Tribe of Indians told me about the original Delaware store that still stands in Linwood, so we slow down and read street signs. I appreciate her emailed directions today as we scrutinize the houses, many of which date to the 1860s. Most of the town's original buildings have additions that are historically haphazard. The trading post is one of them—an upper story has been added to half of the house. Without help we would have never recognized it. We stop to take a photograph of the characteristic front porch with the roof overhang. This is one of the few relics of Delaware history. We are disappointed at how the addition destroys the lines of the building.

At the edge of town we follow a dead-end road and find Stranger Creek, close to its confluence with the Kaw and surprisingly wide. A railroad bridge spans it, and as we watch, a train of coal cars hurtles by. Somewhere owners continue to reap profits from land once acquired from the Delawares.

Next is the site of Lenape, but little appears to remain but fields until we find a road over the tracks. Down the incline we find a collection of old farmhouses. They resemble historic photographs, but I cannot be sure. When I was young, I would not hesitate to stop at a country house and inquire. People were always welcome to visit. After *In Cold Blood* and other random tragedies, people are suspicious of strangers. We keep moving.

Finally, we find the Lenape Cemetery, a square of precious farmland preserved despite the passage of time and the high price of land. The hillside has a range of gravesite markers, ornate to simple, including fieldstones. Some tablet-shaped marble stones are quite old. I am surprised to find the name Bare on several tombstones. This is one of the archaic spellings of my Bair or Bear family. Henry Bare's stone has an image of shaking hands. Perhaps this is a mason's symbol or a welcome to heaven or a last handshake. It is not overtly Christian, like the crosses on other markers. It is identical to the tombstone for the Delaware leader Black Beaver at Fort Sill, Oklahoma. Beaver is another of my family names in the cemetery, a husband and wife.

We walk through the hillside lots and find names like Allen, Boaz, Burnett, Cullison, and McConnell. Fresh mounds of dirt show this remote rural cemetery still receives souls from the surrounding community. The dates and names and a few images are all that commemorate these people's lives. We finish our walk through the aisles and leave.

We continue southward across the river to Eudora, a town named after a Shawnee man's daughter. Here we find the historic Delaware cemetery, the Zeigler Cemetery. The fenced lot filled with cedars has more direct ties to tribal history. A plaque recounts, "The Retsingers deeded the land for the cemetery in the 1870s so Delaware Indians who lived in this area from 1829 to 1866–67 would have a burial place." When these Delaware people smoked their prayers every evening along the Kaw River, they left these words, etched on the cemetery marker: "We will have peace as long as the moon will rise and set on the Kaw." Their breath mixed with mist, and so they commingled with the river. Their bones became part of the land. Names include Adair, "Carl 'the Chief' Koerner," "Colored man, name unknown," Longacre, Matthew, Retsinger, Schultz, Swisher, and Zeigler. The earliest burial is 1833, and the latest is 1944. Farmers and relatives in the area keep the cemetery neatly mown. My husband and I leave tobacco at the cemetery gate and finally turn to the road home. Another cemetery in Kansas City holds Delaware leaders like Captain Ketchum and his family, but the quick winter twilight is turning to night.

The history of Delaware people may seem to be fading farther into the past. Yet the dice roll and fortunes change. On July 10, 2013, the Delaware Tribe of Indians, of Bartlesville, Oklahoma, purchased eighty-seven acres of the North Lawrence farm where the Big House once stood. They have no plans for the land yet, but Delawares renew their ties to former Kansas holdings. On the way back to the highway my husband and I pass a small sign that identifies the land.

Delawares endured the longest Trail of Tears among Native nations, extending from the 1600s to 1867 and from the Atlantic Ocean to Oklahoma. The resulting diaspora of Delaware bands is a direct aftermath. Each place on that route retains importance to Delaware people, including these Kansas lands. Most important is the presence of the Kaw River, still a major source of water for people. The valleys continue to be transportation routes for trains and highway traffic. Whenever I look north from my house to the river, I see the Delaware history as a road that starts in the distant past and travels along the Kaw River and continues.

❖

Native writers of the twentieth century and into the twenty-first create literary works that reflect on Native identities in their myriad forms, from "blood quantum," a measure usually restricted to animal breeds, to cultural experience. These authors create a virtual community, expanded by social media. This is a new haven as Delawares and other Native people disperse geographically in a country where mobility is often essential to livelihood. Over 70 percent of American Indians and Alaska Natives live away from tribal communities, according to the 2010 U.S. Census. Native people are among the most mobile of United States citizens. They journey to homelands for tribal dances, and they follow the powwow trail, which leads all over the country.

Prose writer Louis Owens uses the term *blood trails*, which also defines Native people, especially mixed-bloods. The migrations of forced removal, for Owens the Cherokee Trail of Tears, parallel heritage, or "bloodline-related," experiences. One aspect is the reconfiguring of original literatures, which is "another kind of removal." Even Native groups that did not lose their lands struggle to adapt to the English language. Their stories do not fit easily into United States mainstream culture. All Native people live in at least two worlds, usually more.

Delaware journeys away from a geographic homeland—through Pennsylvania, Ohio, Wisconsin or Indiana, Missouri, and Kansas—are a series of dislocations. The original center place, the New Jersey shore region, is more than a physical point. It is a moment of coherence, a place and time when narratives corresponded most directly to people's environment. The farther away from this point, the more individuals struggle to create new survival stories. Sometimes the struggle is creative, sometimes tragic.

Diaspora is also an internalized process. Sometimes the process of fragmentation becomes the new tradition. In government and church boarding schools for American Indians and Alaska Natives, many students were forcibly separated from their families. They were beaten by staff. In turn they began beating their children, introducing a new practice because that is what they learned. My grandparents avoided the boarding schools and problems associated with them by staying outside of the federal jurisdiction. This did not prevent a legacy of broken histories. My mother separated herself from her parents and extended family.

My grandfather disappeared periodically and rode the rails, inexplicable lapses from his responsibilities. My brother remembers his calls from California or Oregon, half a continent away. These distant destinations, I discovered through census records, were not impulsive wanderings but, instead, corresponded to places where his maternal cousins lived. One owned an orchard in Oregon, where Grandfather could find seasonal work. On his travels he tried to keep contact with a dispersed family, an impossible task but one he attempted. He could not, however, articulate this quest to even his most intimate family members.

Owens's family retained some oral history and lost more. When he wrote about his experiences, he suffered public attacks for his mixed identity, yet he relayed an important story about a large population of Native-descended people. His eventual suicide was a tragic loss. This final choice is the most extreme form of silence.

Silence is a common symptom of the trauma of Native displacement. Chickasaw author Linda Hogan writes about the "unnamed grief" her family experienced as the family lived in a complicated, urbanized, and difficult world: "As a young person coming from silences of both family and history, I had little of the language I needed to put a human life together. I was inarticulate to voice it, therefore to know it, even from within. I had an unnamed grief not only my own." Hogan's "silence of both family and history" describes my own experience. My family mostly suppressed controversial histories of the past, except for rare private conversations like those my brother and I had with my grandfather. I presume they occurred with my father as well, since he changed political allegiances. Never were these topics discussed openly with the entire family. The incident that precipitated the family move to Kansas City, at the height of Ku Klux Klan activity, is only briefly sketched. Stories of other Native-descended people in the region create some context. In Oklahoma, a few miles south of my Bruner great-grandparents' homes, Jeanetta Calhoun Mish describes terrifying vigilante activity, including lynchings. This Delaware writer's accounts include attacks on Native people as well as African Americans. John D. Berry recounts the 1930s story of his mother, then in second grade, telling her class she was Indian. That night neighbors shot up the house and forced the family to move.

In public schools and mainstream media I learned a conqueror's narrative that erased surviving Native people, including Delawares, who persist long after the Manhattan Island days. Like Hogan, I grew up inarticulate and barely able to be understood when I dared speak aloud. Like Hogan, I discovered some lost threads through the medium of the written language. She describes the empowerment of language: "One day the words came. I was an adult. I went to school after work. I read. I wrote. Words came, anchored to the earth, to matter, to the wholeness of nature. There was, in this, a fall, this time to holy ground of a different order, a present magic, a light-bearing, soul-saving presence that illuminated my heart and mind and altered my destiny." Reading and writing help me learn the "wholeness of nature." I wish my grandfather were alive now to appreciate the shared community of other Native peoples who find ways to speak. Writers help me sort out possibilities. Gerald Vizenor's "fourth dimension" is another axis that informs wholeness, a historic accounting of experience. He uses mapping as a more precise documentation of history—"virtual cartography." He describes how the past is a presence, beyond language, memory, and culture. It exists within the present as "transmotion." This is a distinctly Native idea of time and history, and it helps me find peace in a town where the past is so visible.

I honor the lives my relatives endured by learning as much as I can about them. I will pass forward a larger story, and in the stream of time I hear more stories. They add to a more complete counter-narrative.

Land is a continuous anchor. Some cloudy mornings the hillside where I live slips backward in time. Again it is a large farm with vast fields, not houses. Cattle are outside the window, and then it shifts backward again to the time of the Oregon Trail. My house sits squarely on the former trail. My husband swears he hears people moving about when it is dark. I imagine that time and before. I see the slope, the slight depression where water collects, and the tiny rill that becomes a headwaters during rainstorms. In winter snow covers everything except the roll of land against sky and bluestem grass. This is what is most real. My grandfather joins me. We exist connected to the unfailing elements beyond words—soil, water, air, and sun.

❖

When Native and European people met at L'Anse aux Meadows, about the year 1000, already a protocol for trading existed—the Native inhabitants had furs to offer, and they wanted guns in exchange. At first language was a problem, but then, without explanation from the chronicler, they communicate. Indigenous Newfoundland people trade for milk instead of weapons. This is the first recorded incident of contact. Because of the established trading etiquette, they must have had previous meetings. Europeans and North Americans are not opposing, partitioned people. Interconnections have occurred beyond recorded times. But this moment at L'Anse aux Meadows is a written record in the greater shared history.

Another first contact is a toddler's encounter with mysterious objects, like magnets. My grandson came to visit yesterday. His blond hair sticks up all over, so his mother cuts it in a Mohawk. He is an adorable little man—Menominee, German, and Irish on his mother's side and Lakota, Norwegian, and German on his father's side. His hair will darken as he grows older. Although both his parents are tribal members, he is eligible only for descendancy status in the Menominee Nation, not formal membership. The politics of identity are complex and often exclude people with Native heritage and history, like my grandfather and like this little boy.

My grandson has not visited for a month, and he has a moment of surprise as he recognizes his surroundings. He runs to his favorite corners: the aromatic shelf where coffee is stored; the cupboard of plastic bowls; and the playroom of stuffed teddy bears. His mother is Bear Clan, which he inherits. His name is Keso', the eternal Sun. His ancestor namesake, like the Sun, was not moved from his course easily.

This little bear allows grandparents to bestow some hugs. Then he is again in motion, exercising his mind as well as his sturdy legs. He is interested in magnetism. He and I take large magnets from the refrigerator, not small ones that would be dangerous if swallowed, and then experiment with wood, glass, and paper. He wants to learn. Even though he does not repeat the word *magnet*, he remembers everything.

He collects memories of me, his grandmother, a figure who will shift among many images in his mind and add to his identity. How I hold him, how I speak to him, my squishiness—all of these are mastered already. He looks at me gravely and then shifts attention to novel objects that must be learned. Magnets.

Stories of Delawares in New Jersey and their copper pipes and jewelry are far away, in time and in geography, yet they also are present as we touch a steel measuring cup—which sticks to the magnet. We learn electromagnetism, a powerful force that cannot be seen yet has undeniable strength, like love.

My own grandfather also is present as I watch the youngster's ravenous curiosity. Once, years ago, I first met Grandfather, and at that moment I grafted his presence onto my own sense of self. I have spent the rest of my life with him nearby. His life resonates, along with other ancestors, as I hand Keso' a large green magnet that once held a sage wreath to the front door. He remembers the front door and notices the portability of this green object. His mind is an electrical field like the magnet. Many stories orbit. Some will stick.

In warm months his family will take him on hikes and teach him to touch and taste rocks, distinguish the color patterns of sunfish, smell the lairs of chipmunks, and translate the chatter of squirrels. In this way the boy will learn subtleties possible through his senses. With his eyes, hands, and nose, he will learn mulberries, sunflowers, elderberries, echinacea, mullein, yarrow, and the square stems of mints. He will hear about the Water Being that lives in the spring across the river from his great-grandmother's house on the Menominee reservation. He will attend school and learn addition tables and writing. Most of all he will learn habits of observation and how to relish each moment. This style of approaching experience continues the tradition handed down for generations, whatever language is used.

As I touch my grandson's hand, I also touch my grandfather's hand. I remember how he lifted me when I was a child. I remember his aroma of aftershave, tobacco, and damp hair. His flannel shirt is scratchy like his whiskers. His eyes are soft. Each memory is the first time I have ever seen him. This is the grandparent who talked to me seriously and entrusted me with important teachings. My poet grandmother of British Isles and German heritage also shaped my future, and I am grateful to her as well. The influences blend together, not as opposing forces.

If only I could end the story here, with the cycle of losses healed through magical memories and the life of this grandchild. In a European fairy tale this is the "happily ever after" moment, closure. Instead, I must be truthful and report a continuing cycle. Too frequently, my extended family sends news of children lost to despair and addiction, like my niece.

My Cherokee friend Linda Rodriguez gives me permission to describe a family story, and I could recount dozens more from personal experience. Linda's Cherokee grandmother was denigrated by her daughter-in-law. The non-Native mother hid letters and gifts intended for Linda. The girl was not allowed to visit the beloved elder. That negativity, however, did not prevent Linda from treasuring the memories she did have of her grandmother, nor did it prevent her from recuperating her birthright. She has become a powerful Cherokee writer and person.

Some reconnections occurred after I began researching my grandfather's story. Cousins sent stories about our family, and we reflected on how our parents and grandparents responded to historic patterns as well as they could. Even distant cousins reported eerily similar stories, and the shared narrative is comforting. They confirmed the Native identity and offered more photographs. People my parents never allowed into family discussions came to life through these conversations.

This process has healed me. I better understand my mother's barely suppressed anger in terms of generalized cultural trauma, not personal failings. Bitterness eases. I ask my husband if he notices any difference since I began this inquiry into my grandfather's past. "You enjoy things more," he says. His perspective surprises me, but yes, the shared stories help me feel a deeper range of joy. Humor is funnier. I am more able to shake off criticism and more able to focus. I now see myself as a flawed yet valued person in my family and communities. Flaws are part of the process, not irrevocable impediments.

My grandfather was absent most of my childhood. He had imperfect, sometimes broken relationships with his parents, his brothers, his cousins, his daughter, and his grandchildren. Nonetheless, he left an important legacy. He sustained his marriage through fifty years and never deserted his family through abandonment or suicide. He taught an attitude to words, the importance of language and stories. He valued history as a continuing aspect of daily experience. He stayed true to a homeland, the Kansas prairies where skies, rivers, winds, and the earth's body rearrange themselves daily in intense colors and forms. This is the source of our breath, blood, bones, and flesh. Those of us descended from Frank Bruner have a living connection to his life.

❖

My grandfather probably never knew his Delaware traditions from the Atlantic Seaboard. Delaware elders tell me that most oral tradition of that time is gone. Colonial documents preserve suggestions of the Delaware past, from a European settler point of view. Historic silence has been the fate of the overwhelmed Delaware peoples, so most of our history is absent from the national narrative. A few borrow words from Algonquian languages survive: *moccasin, powwow, persimmon,* and *terrapin.*

Many of today's Delawares are Turtle band. The land turtle group went south to Oklahoma, an elder told me, and the water turtle group went north to the woodlands, a land of lakes and rivers. In both places Delawares thrive.

Turtles are hard to kill. Their hearts keep beating long after separation from their bodies. I met an Arikara woman whose grandmother once gave her a beating heart to swallow, along with broth. This was an old ceremony for a woman's coming of age. The woman never forgot the lesson of Turtle's strength, as she felt the sensation of the moving heart in her mouth, throat, stomach, and gut. She still enjoys a long life.

Turtles survive because of their strong hearts and also because they can adapt to many environments. English has three categories for turtles: tortoise, a sea dweller; land turtle; and terrapin, for freshwater turtles. Delaware language points to yet more niches for Turtles. Bands within the Turtle Clan are "Bark Country," "Beggar," "Brave," and "Snapping." The words suggest rich narratives of geographies, behaviors, and turtle species like the snapping turtle.

Anyone who fishes muddy inland rivers has stories of great snapping turtles that clamp bait and cannot be removed. I have met people who have lost fingertips.

In my early teens I enjoyed the solitude of fishing in a small lake formed from an oxbow of the Neosho River. This was one of the gifts of a Flint Hills upbringing. I spent hours wandering the lake, marveling at sunfish colors, dragonflies, and placid painted turtles. I caught stringers of pan fish and cleaned them for my mother.

One day I tossed in my line beyond the range of snags and watched the bobber tip in the current. Suddenly, an underwater fury attacked the worm. I pulled hard against an unseen surge of power. Finally, I could see the prehistoric beast's razor-sharp talons and beak. I did not know this kind of animal existed, but I knew I was outmatched. I cut the line.

I remember that first snapping turtle as though it were still next to me and its ferocity. I remember my Delaware grandfather's power. Turtles can be both dormant and active, like memory itself. When turtles burrow into mud in the winter, they wait but do not die. They have their seasons and migrations.

Turtles help me understand my own identity. Recently, a non-Native friend asked me why a minority of my own heritage should make any difference. Shouldn't the majority of my bloodline sources, she reasoned, be my sole identity? She followed a majority rule paradigm, which subtracts the lesser sum and discards it.

To answer, I used an example from my Menominee husband's experiences as a deer hunter. He explained to me how exact fractions seldom exist in nature. When hunters apportion a deer's quarters, the shoulders and haunches differ. Also, the heart beats extra blood to the dominant side, so that half is larger. No fourth is equal. This exemplifies the issue of blood quantum, or abstract fractionalization of Native ancestry for federal "Indian preference" regulations. Many tribal membership requirements echo this federal model. A deer or a turtle or even a human may be quartered, but living beings are not symmetrical masses. Like a turtle, a human's single heart is critical to existence, no matter which quarter holds it.

In overt and subtle ways my grandfather's intangible teachings impact my family profoundly, first through his direct descendants, my mother and her brother. Further, he changed the course of my father's life, in terms of occupation, political identity, and religion. Like a turtle's enduring heartbeat, my family has a living legacy no matter how far we live from the Atlantic or how long ago Delawares and Dutch formed a trade alliance on Manhattan Island. We are thankful for the land, wherever we live, and the food that ties us to it. We listen to our hearts, which are always at the center.

Notes

I. A TWENTIETH-CENTURY NATIVE MAN

4   *His ancestor William Walker*: Connelley, "Kansas City, Kansas."

9   *I realize, after Obermeyer's talk*: Douglass, *History of Wayne County, Ohio*, 161.

13   *Diné (Navajo) poet Luci Tapahonso*: *Blue Horses Rush In*, xiv.

18–19   *"Old Man came from the south"*: Chewing Black Bones, "Blackfeet Creation Tale."

26   *The local histories*: Bruner, *Days to Remember*; Handle, Clark, and Obee, *Burns, Kans.*

26   *"Mrs. F. L. Bruner presented"*: *Burns Monitor*, quoted in Bruner, *Days to Remember*, 29.

28   *"Among those who developed"*: Mooney, *History of Butler County*, 113.

29   *"children chose it as a favorite"*: Jensen, "Passing Era of a Kansas Small Town," 80.

29   *"Chauquecake"*: Howe, *Historical Collections of Ohio*.

32   *From beadwork designs*: Lyford, *Ojibwa Crafts (Chippewa)*, 142.

33   *"double curve" design*: Speck, *Double-Curve Motif*.

33   *These stems are a type*: Mihku Paul, private conversation, 2012; Tantamidgeon and Fawcett, "Basketry Designs," 135.

35   *Later I will find*: Speck, *Double-Curve Motif*.

39   *After 1900*: Yost, "History of Lynchings in Kansas."

44   *The Ku Klux Klan became a major threat*: Sloan, "Kansas Battles the Invisible Empire."

48 *Moulton also had*: *Reports of Cases Argued and Determined.*

58 *Gretchen Eick, a Wichita*: Gretchen Eick, email message to author, August 20, 2013.

58 *A 1782 mob killing*: Farrar, "Moravian Massacre."

66 *"Chief," as he was called*: "Frank Lindley," in Buller, *Can't You Hear the Whistle Blowing*, 9–20.

76 *A checklist of historic trauma*: Wesley-Esquimaux and Smolewski, *Aboriginal Historic.* An early scholar in the field is Judith Hermann (*Trauma and Recovery*). Scholars who identify "a legacy of chronic trauma and unresolved grief across generations" for American Indians are Maria Y. H. Brave Heart and Lemyra M. DeBruyn ("American Indian Holocaust," 60).

2. CUTTING TIES

85 *This patchwork of communities*: Perry and Skolnick, *Keeper of the Delaware Dolls*, 51.

85 *Delaware tribal member Lynette Perry*: Perry and Skolnick, *Keeper*, 64.

91 *eastern edge of the Flint Hills*: With, King, and Jensen, "Remaining Large Grasslands," 3152.

95 *Gregory Orr writes about*: Orr, *Poetry*, 4.

102 *Dolls were fed ceremonial*: Jones, *History of the Ojibwey Indians*, 111–15.

102 *Lynette Perry describes how*: Perry and Skolnick, *Keeper*, 202.

103 *My sister and I*: Perry and Skolnick, *Keeper*, 202.

106 *An area seed keeper*: Dianna Henry, email message to the author, December 19, 2011.

107 *"Delicious cakes were baked"*: Johnson, *Wonder-Working Providence*, 1654.

107 *In 1683 William Penn*: Penn, Letter to the Free Society of Traders.

110 *Leslie Marmon Silko writes*: Silko, *Turquoise Ledge*, 226.

3. A HAUNTED LIFE

123 *One Delaware game*: Bragdon, *Native People*, 222.

124 *Delawares had a dice game*: Bragdon, *Native People*, 222–23.

124–25 *Louise Erdrich writes about*: Erdrich, *Bingo Palace*, 143.

136 *"No person was anywhere"*: Stafford, *You Must Revise Your Life*, 8.

139 *"Upon hearing that a parent"*: "History." *Ramapough Lunaape Nation*

139 *"They lived in longhouses"*: Bruchac, *Roots of Survival*, 190.

144 *Geary Hobson, a professor*: Hobson, "Folks Left Out," 344–49.

146 *American Indigenous people have*: "Fast Facts for Youth in Indian Country."

4. TODAY

153 *"rectangular in ground-plan"*: Harrington, "Preliminary Sketch of Lenápe Culture," 217.

154 *They used deep-bowled spoons*: Harrington, "Vestiges of Material Culture," 408.

155 *A record by a government agent*: "Abstract of Stock Stolen by Whites." Although the abstract title suggests a longer period, the original document only covers three months.

155 *"In a treaty"*: Ewing, *Early History of North Lawrence*, 8.

155 *One oral tradition story*: Caron, "Tribe Has Historical Ties."

155 *The Delaware "big house"*: Caron, "Tribe Has Historical Ties"; Speck, *Study of the Delaware Indian Big House Ceremony*, 17.

156 *"Of a total of 201"*: Nichols and Hauptman, "Delaware,"

156 *A former coach at Haskell*: Castaneda, "Cliff McDonald Tells the Story."

157 *He was re-christened*: "Linwood History."

157 *A woman from the Kansas*: Gloria White, email message to the author, November 15, 2015.

158 *After* in Cold Blood: Truman Capote, *In Cold Blood*. New York: Random House, 1966.

158 *It is identical*: "Black Beaver," Findagrave.com, http://www .findagrave.com/cgi-bin/fg.cgi?page=gr&GRid=1210.

158 *"The Retsingers deeded"*: "Delaware Cemetery," *Eudora History*.

159 *On July 10, 2013*: "Purchase of Property in Lawrence," 1.

159 *Over 70 percent*: Norris, Vines, and Hoeffel, "American Indian and Alaska Native Population," 20.

160 *Prose writer Louis Owens*: Owens, *Mixedblood Messages*, 150–51.

161 *"As a young person"*: Hogan, *Woman Who Watches Over the World*, 56.

161 *In Oklahoma, a few miles*: Mish, *Oklahomeland*, 101–24.

161 *John D. Berry*: Berry, "Mixed Blood."

162 *"One day the words"*: Hogan, *Woman Who Watches*, 57.

162 *Gerald Vizenor's "fourth dimension"*: Vizenor, *Fugitive Poses*, 167–81. Vizenor reviews his ideas about Indigenous transmotion, cartography, and survivance in this section of the book.

163 *When Native and European*: Magnusson and Palsson, *Vinland Sagas*.

165 *My Cherokee friend Linda*: Rodriguez, public reading, Oak Park Public Library.

Bibliography

Few Delaware oral accounts remain from the earliest days. Names were Anglicized in the seventeenth century and after. Some of the early commentators, such as Reverend Peter Jones, were mixed-blood—his mother was Eastern Ojibwa.

"Abstract of Stock Stolen by Whites from the Delaware Tribe of Indians since the Treaty of 1854." Pratt Papers, Kansas Historical Society Research Center at Topeka. Roll 9, beginning frame 391, October–December 1862. *Lenape Delaware History*. ftp://lenapedelaware history.net/mirror/stock_stolen.htm.

Adams, Richard C. *Legends of the Delaware Indians and Picture Writing*. Edited by Deborah Nichols. Syracuse: Syracuse University Press, 1997.

Berry, John D. "Mixed Blood: Connecting Two Worlds." Panel presentation, Returning the Gift Conference. Albuquerque. December 4, 2015.

Besaw, Rhonda. "Rhonda Besaw: Traditional Abenaki Artist." *Bead Society of Great Britain* 97 (Fall 2009): 15–19.

Black Beaver. Photograph. *Lenape Delaware History*. ftp://lenapedelaware history.net/mirror/bioa-g.htm.

Bragdon, Kathleen J. *Native People of Southern New England, 1500–1650*. Norman: University of Oklahoma Press, 1996.

Brave Heart, Maria Y. H., and Lemyra M. DeBruyn. "The American Indian Holocaust: Healing Historical Unresolved Grief." *American Indian and Alaska Native Mental Health Research* 8, no. 2 (1998): 60–82.

Bruchac, Joseph. *Roots of Survival: Native American Storytelling and the Sacred*. Golden: Fulcrum Publishing, 1996.

Bruner, Hazel C. *Days to Remember: The Burns Community, 1864–1970*. North Newton KS: Mennonite Press, 1970.

Buller, Curtis, ed. *Can't You Hear the Whistle Blowing? A History of Newton High School Basketball, 1900–1958 & 1979*. Denver: Sid Gates, 2008.

Caron, Michael. "Tribe Has Historical Ties to Land." *Lawrence Journal-World*, August 14, 2013. *Delaware Tribe*. http://delawaretribe.org /blog/2013/10/01/opinion-tribe-has-historical-ties-to-land/.

Castaneda, Erin. "Cliff McDonald Tells the Story of Teepee Junction." *Lawrence Journal World*, November 5, 2008. LJWorld.com. http:// www2.ljworld.com/videos/sets/2008/nov/06/cliff _mcdonald_tells_story_teepee_junction/.

Chewing Black Bones. "Blackfeet Creation Tale." In *Indian Legends from the Northern Rockies*, edited by Ella E. Clark. *Montana Tribes*. http://montanatribes.org/links_&_resources/tribes/Blackfeet.pdf.

Connelley, William E. "Kansas City, Kansas: Its Place in the History of the State." Paper read before the Wyandotte County Historical Society, Kansas City, April 4, 1918. Reprint. Kansas City: John Brown Press, 2010.

Cutler, William. *History of the State of Kansas*. Chicago: A. T. Andreas, 1883. *Kansas Collection Books*. http://www.kancoll.org/books/cutler/.

"Delaware Cemetery." *Eudora, KS, History*. http://eudorakshistory.com /cemeteries/area-cemeteries.htm.

Douglass, Ben. *History of Wayne County, Ohio, from the Days of the First Pioneers and Settlers to the Present Time*. Indianapolis: Robert Douglass, 1878. https://archive.org/details/cu31924028848765.Eick, Gretchen. Email message to the author. Aug. 20, 2013.

Erdrich, Louise. *The Bingo Palace*. New York: Harper Perennial, 1994.

Ewing, A. B., ed. *Early History of North Lawrence*. Lawrence KS: Wood-lawn Parent Teachers Association, 1961.

Farrar, William. "The Moravian Massacre: A Paper Read at the Sixth Annual Meeting of the Society at Columbus." *Ohio Journal*. http://publications.ohiohistory.org/ohj/search/display php?page =7&ipp=20&searchterm=Array&vol=3&pages=261-315.

"Fast Facts for Youth in Indian Country." *Aspen Institute*. http://www
.aspeninstitute.org/sites/default/files/content/images/Fast%20
Facts.pdf.

Fawcett, Melissa Jayne. *The Lasting of the Mohegans: The Story of the Wolf
People*. Uncasville CT: Mohegan Tribe, 1995.

Fitzgerald, Stephanie. "Mohegan Wood-Splint Baskets." In *Early Native
Literacies in New England: A Documentary and Critical Anthology*,
edited by Kristina Bross and Hilary E. Wyss, 51–56. Amherst:
University of Massachusetts Press, 2008.

Handle, Marjorie, Norma Clark, and Marie Obee, eds. *Burns, Kans.: 100-
Years, 1880–1980*. Burns KS: Burns Centennial Staff, 1980.

Harrington, M. R. "A Preliminary Sketch of Lenápe Culture." *American
Anthropologist*, n.s. 15 (1913): 208–35. http://www.jstor.org
/stable/659665?seq=6#page_scan_tab_contents.

———. "Vestiges of Material Culture among the Canadian Delawares."
American Anthropologist, n.s. 10, no. 3 (1908): 408–18. http://
onlinelibrary.wiley.com/doi/10.1525/aa.1908.10.3.02a00040/pdf.

Hermann, Judith. *Trauma and Recovery: The Aftermath of Violence, from
Domestic Abuse to Political Terror*. Ann Arbor: University of Michigan
Press, 1992.

Henry, Dianna. Email message to the author. December 19, 2011.

"History." *Ramapough Lunaape Nation*. http://www.ramapoughlenape
nation.org/history.

Hobson, Geary. "The Folks Left Out of the Photographs." In *The People
Who Stayed: Southeastern Indian Writing after Removal*, edited by
Geary Hobson, Janet McAdams, and Kathryn Walkiewicz. Norman:
University of Oklahoma Press, 2010.

Hogan, Linda. *The Woman Who Watches Over the World: A Native Memoir*. New York: Norton, 2002.

Howe, Henry. *Historical Collections of Ohio in Two Volumes*. Cincinnati: C.
J. Krehbiel & Co., 1888. Google ebook. https://archive.org/details
/historicalcollec01inhowe.

Johnson, Edward. *The Wonder-Working Providence of Sion's Savior in New
England*, bk. 2, chap. 6. N.p., 1654. Ancestry.com. http://rootsweb
.ancestry.com/~usgenweb/special/history/providence/2chap1-10.htm.

Jones, Peter. *History of the Ojebway Indians with Especial Reference to Their
Conversion to Christianity: With a Brief Memoir of the Writer by
Peter Jones (Kahkewaquonaby); and Introductory Notice by G. Osborn*.

London: A. W. Bennett, 1861. https://openlibrary.org/books
/OL7213189M/History_of_the_Ojebway_Indians.

"Linwood History." *United States School District 458.* http://www.usd458
.org/gen/blvs/Linwood_History_p44.html.

Longtoe, Vera. "The Double Curve Motif." *Elnu Abenaki Tribe.* http://
www.elnuabenakitribe.org/DoubleCurves.html.

Lyford, Carrie A. *Ojibwa Crafts (Chippewa).* U.S. Department of the Inte-
rior, Bureau of Indian Affairs, 1943.

Magnusson, Magnus, and Hermann Palsson, trans. *The Vinland Sagas:
Norse Discovery of America.* New York: Penguin, 1965. Kindle edition.

Mish, Jeanetta Calhoun. *Oklahomeland: Essays.* Beaumont TX: Lamar
University Press, 2015.

Mooney, Vol. P. *History of Butler County, Kansas.* Lawrence KS: Standard
Publishing, 1916. *KSGenWeb Project.* http://www.ksgenweb.org
/archives/butler/history/1916/.

Nichols, Deborah, and Laurence M. Hauptman. "The Delaware: Warriors for the Union." In *Civil War Times.* Historynet.com. http://
www.upa.pdx.edu/IMS/currentprojects/TAHv3/Content/PDFs
/Delaware_Warriors_Union.pdf.

Norris, Tina, Paula L. Vines, and Elizabeth M. Hoeffel. "American Indian
and Alaska Native Population: 2010: Census Briefs." *U.S. Census
Bureau.* January 2012. http://www.census.gov/prod/cen2010/briefs
/c2010br-10.pdf.

Orr, Gregory. *Poetry as Survival.* Athens: University of Georgia Press,
2002.

Owens, Louis. *Mixedblood Messages: Literature, Film, Family, Place.* Norman: University of Oklahoma, 1998.

Paul, Mihku. *The Work of Mihku Paul: Waponahki Poet and Artist.* http://
mihkupaul.com/.

Penn, William. Letter to the Free Society of Traders in London. Philadelphia, August 16, 1683. In *The Life of William Penn, with Selections
from His Correspondence and Autobiography*, by Samuel M. Janney,
6th ed. Philadelphia: Friends' Book Association, 1882. *U.S. History.*
http://www.ushistory.org/penn/penn_journey.htm.

"Purchase of Property in Lawrence, Kansas." *Delaware Tribe of Indians.*
http://delawaretribe.org/wp-content/uploads/Lawrence-Property-
Purchase-1a.pdf.

Reports of Cases Argued and Determined in the Supreme Court of Kansas.
Vol. 52. Topeka: Kansas State Printing, 1893. Google ebook.

Rodriguez, Linda. Public reading, Oak Park Public Library, July 21, 2015.

Silko, Leslie Marmon. *The Turquoise Ledge*. New York: Viking, 2010.

Sloan, Charles William, Jr. "Kansas Battles the Invisible Empire: The Legal Ouster of the KKK from Kansas, 1922–1927." *Kansas History* 40, no. 3 (1974): 393–409. http://www.kshs.org/p/kansas-battles-the -invisible-empire/13247.

Speck, Frank G. *The Double-Curve Motif in Northeastern Algonquin Art*. Ottawa: Government Printing Bureau, 1914.

———. *A Study of the Delaware Indian Big House Ceremony*. Harrisburg: [Pennsylvania Historical Commission], 1931). Hathitrust.org. http:// babel.hathitrust.org/cgi/pt?id=mdp.39015002692252;view=1up ;seq=6.

Stafford, William. *You Must Revise Your Life*. Ann Arbor: University of Michigan Press, 1986.

Tantamidgeon, Gladys, and Melissa Jayne Fawcett. "Basketry Designs." In *Key into the Language of Woodsplint Baskets*, edited by Russell G. Handsman and Ann McMullen. Washington CT: American Archaeological Institute, 1987.

Tapahonso, Luci. *Blue Horses Rush In*. Tucson: University of Arizona Press, 1997.

Vizenor, Gerald. *Fugitive Poses: Native American Indian Scenes of Absence and Presence*. Lincoln: University of Nebraska Press, 2000.

Wesley-Esquimaux, Cynthia C., and Magdalena Smolewski. *Aboriginal Historic Trauma and Aboriginal Healing, Prepared for the Aboriginal Healing Foundation*. Ottawa: Aboriginal Healing Foundation, 2004. http://www.ahf.ca/downloads/historic-trauma.pdf.

White, Gloria. Email message to the author, November 15, 2015.

With, Kimberly A., Anthony W. King, and William E. Jensen. "Remaining Large Grasslands May Not Be Sufficient to Prevent Grassland Bird Declines." *Biological Conservation* 141 (2008): 3152. http://www.fws.gov/southwest/es/documents/R2ES/LitCited /LPC_2012/With_et_al_2008.pdf.

Yost, Genevieve. "History of Lynchings in Kansas." *Kansas Historical Quarterly* 2, no. 2 (May 1933): 182–219. Kansas State Historical Society. https://www.kshs.org/p/kansas-historical-quarterly-history -of-lynchings-in-kansas/12580.

First to Fight
By Henry Mihesuah
Edited by Devon Abbott Mihesuah

Mourning Dove: A Salishan Autobiography
Edited by Jay Miller

I'll Go and Do More: Annie Dodge Wauneka, Navajo Leader and Activist
By Carolyn Niethammer

Tales of the Old Indian Territory and Essays on the Indian Condition
By John Milton Oskison
Edited by Lionel Larré

Elias Cornelius Boudinot: A Life on the Cherokee Border
By James W. Parins

John Rollin Ridge: His Life and Works
By James W. Parins

Singing an Indian Song: A Biography of D'Arcy McNickle
By Dorothy R. Parker

Crashing Thunder: The Autobiography of an American Indian
Edited by Paul Radin

Turtle Lung Woman's Granddaughter
By Delphine Red Shirt
and Lone Woman

Telling a Good One: The Process of a Native American Collaborative Biography
By Theodore Rios and
Kathleen Mullen Sands

William W. Warren: The Life, Letters, and Times of an Ojibwe Leader
By Theresa M. Schenck

Sacred Feathers: The Reverend Peter Jones (Kahkewaquonaby) and the Mississauga Indians
By Donald B. Smith

Grandmother's Grandchild: My Crow Indian Life
By Alma Hogan Snell
Edited by Becky Matthews
Foreword by Peter Nabokov

No One Ever Asked Me: The World War II Memoirs of an Omaha Indian Soldier
By Hollis D. Stabler
Edited by Victoria Smith

Blue Jacket: Warrior of the Shawnees
By John Sugden

Muscogee Daughter: My Sojourn to the Miss America Pageant
By Susan Supernaw
Foreword by Geary Hobson

I Tell You Now: Autobiographical Essays by Native American Writers
Edited by Brian Swann
and Arnold Krupat

Postindian Conversations
By Gerald Vizenor and A. Robert Lee

Chainbreaker: The Revolutionary War Memoirs of Governor Blacksnake
As told to Benjamin Williams
Edited by Thomas S. Abler

Standing in the Light: A Lakota Way of Seeing
By Severt Young Bear and R. D. Theisz

Sarah Winnemucca
By Sally Zanjani

To order or obtain more information on these or other University of Nebraska Press titles, visit www.nebraskapress.unl.edu.